FHF

Friends
Homosexual
Fellowship

Meeting Gay Friends

**Essays by
gay Quakers**

**Edited by John Banks
and Martina Weitsch
with an afterword by
Mary D E Guillemard**

First published 1982 by Friends Homosexual Fellowship
Second impression 1985

ISBN 0 9508031 0 3

Meeting gay friends.
  1. Homosexuality
  I. Weitsch, Martina   II. Banks, John
  III. Friends Homosexual Fellowship
  261.8'35766   BT708

This book has been typed by Jennifer Barraclough,
designed by Jeremy Greenwood and printed in Great Britain
by Printfine Ltd, Gibraltar Row, King Edward Industrial
Estate, Liverpool L3 7HJ

Further details of Friends Homosexual Fellowship from
Michael Hutchinson, 110 Northfield Road, Birmingham B30 1JG

Further copies of this book may be obtained from
FRIENDS BOOK CENTRE, FRIENDS HOUSE, EUSTON ROAD, LONDON NW1

Foreword

This book represents, as does Quaker writing generally, the
testimony of individuals. The contributors to it are mostly
members of the Religious Society of Friends or attenders
at its meetings. They are also gay. By choosing to consider,
often in intimate detail, the significance of these two
factors in their lives, the writers are offering a living
response to the demands which faith makes on the whole of
human experience. The Quaker way has always been to approach
life experimentally and undogmatically: not to judge by
pre-determined standards but to respect the many forms
in which 'that of God in every one' may be revealed.

We hope that the book will be a useful contribution to
the debate about gayness among the Churches; but some who
might find it most useful are the many young - and not so
young - women and men who are coming to terms with being
gay, and need not theological tracts or sociological
abstractions but the real experiences of ordinary people
with which they can identify and sympathise. Others may
find in the book a way of sharing in the lives of those
who have been no more than an uncomprehended label to them,
and thus discover a richness in the variety of human
experience which illumines their own.

It has not, however, been an easy process for many of
the contributors to make visible sometimes painful, sometimes exhilarating steps along the road of understanding.
Society as a whole is still apprehensive of the minority
view of any kind, and anonymity is for some the only
safeguard against worse than apprehension; to be identified
as gay could mean the end of certain relationships for them,
or the loss of job and career.

For all of them, the support of Friends Homosexual
Fellowship has been of great importance. This group exists
within the Society of Friends to promote an understanding
of gayness among Friends in general and to break down the
barriers of isolation and loneliness which invisibility can
mean for many gay Friends. It was at a meeting of the North
West regional group of FHF that the idea of this book arose,
and since then we have been grateful for the encouragement
and practical and financial help which have enabled us to
bring the project to fruition.

The book is in no sense a formal pronouncement by FHF,
still less by the Society of Friends as a whole. It is
nonetheless offered in that spirit of truth-seeking which
characterises Quaker witness.

John Banks
Martina Weitsch

April 1982

1 Joyce R Mumford

It started almost as long ago as I can remember, when I
came to prefer listening to the radio dance bands of
Jack Payne and Henry Hall to the aunties and uncles of
Children's Hour at teatime, and found I knew what the
love songs were about - hearts beating fast, I-love-yew
and all that. Only for me it was other girls, not boys.
I was too young for that to bother me.

At school, again, girls - some girls - were magic to me.
I made tentative affectionate approaches, was duly rebuffed,
and kept quiet thereafter. Later I tried buying love with
gifts of sweets, which worked for a time. At twelve I was
on an emotional high with Babs, who exchanged delirious
letters with me when I had measles and later deserted me
for boys. We'd had half a dozen kisses, that was all. None
of my other loves gave me anything. I was always in love
with somebody, but I learned not to talk about it. 'Just
a crush,' my mother would say.

Interest in boys came in my teens, but I had a pretty
lonely wartime - immature, sentimental, and shy. I was
weaned on Hollywood, with all its coy conventions and
inhibitions. My basic infantile curiosity about male ana-
tomy was unsatisfied. My diaries of the time show me still
pursuing women devotedly, but at a distance. I was franti-
cally in love, throughout the war, with a female crooner
who didn't know I existed. If I had heard of lesbians I
confused them, like most people then and many still, with
transsexuals, or else I thought of them as frustrated
spinsters who tried to be like men to compensate for their
lack of success in the female role.

It was not until the war was over and I was twenty-three
that I got to university. That was my big chance to get to
know men, for there were four to every woman. Throughout my
fresher year I was in love with Nancy. She was 'best friend'
to me, but nothing physical, nothing emotional, passed
between us. At the same time, I was falling in love with
Ian. This feeling was quite genuine. It was physical and
it was emotional. We went abroad together, necked on trains
and in fields, and finally made it in a Paris hotel room.
He was the only man I have loved - though I had my experiments - but he dominated my love life completely for several years, during which we finished college, got jobs,
and got married. I hoped I would make a satisfactory wife.

After a bit, I found myself humming happily 'I'm in
love again' - with my secretary, a pink-cheeked laughing
young woman who read St Augustine on the train. 'What of
it?' I argued with myself. 'She doesn't know, it hurts no
one, and it adds spice to my life.' She left to get married.
Another colleague, Lucy, whom I see in retrospect to have
been one of us, paused when one day I referred to a woman
in another department as 'probably lesbian', looked me
straight in the eye and demanded 'Are you a lesbian?'
Lightly and, I like to think, unblushingly, I replied,
'I shouldn't think so,' and looked away. Why did I miss

the obvious comeback: 'Are you?' Soon afterwards, Lucy
visited me at home after I had retired pregnant. It was
nice of her.

While our three children were babies they were successively my lovers. A lot of women do not like admitting this.
Nothing, of course, objectionable. I suckled them, I adored
them. The feeling passed. Ian and I were happy as married
couples should be. I neither wanted nor expected anything
more.

As the children got a little older, I took on part-time
work at home, keeping membership records for a society
and part-editing its magazine. I needed some clerical
help for this, and thus I met Anne, who was half my age
and interested exclusively in men. I thought about her
a lot, dreamed about her (my erotic dreams, which happened
from time to time, were divided pretty evenly between
male and female objects), and even wrote her a poem. I
don't know whether she grasped its meaning. From time to
time, as we listened to the pop music of the early 1960s
together, a current passed between us. Nothing more
tangible.

In about 1968, I went to a weekend discussion conference - one of many that I attended; Ian never discouraged
me from pursuing my own kind of social activities, though
he did not share them. This conference took the form of
a sort of confession session or encounter group. Quite a
lot came up about personal problems. One man announced,
quite early on, that he was homosexual and wore a wig.
After that he said he felt ill and went home. Perhaps -
I can't now recall - our reception of what I now realise
was a brave gesture wasn't accepting enough; we implied
'So what?' My own contribution to the conference was to
remark that I felt I was too happy; one day something
would happen that would shake me. As I said that, I knew
that I was holding back something important, but I did
not feel that I was ready to reveal it, or that the group,
although friendly, was ready to receive it.

Two years and several conferences later, the organiser
asked me to get in touch with a woman who would have
liked to go to the next one but, having a demanding young
family, a full-time job and no husband - he had, humil-
iatingly, abandoned her for a nightclub stripper - had
asked instead for someone to write her an account of it.
I undertook this task and thus began an uninhibited and
joyful correspondence, despite Ian's forebodings about
'getting involved'. In the summer I visited Theodora and
her family. She told me her life story. We drank rough
cider and went to her local Quaker meeting. When we parted,
I hugged and kissed her spontaneously, and in a subsequent
letter she made it clear that she had welcomed that. She
was clearly a woman starved of affection; equally clearly,
this was because a relentlessly critical intellect, and a
lack of tact in expressing her thoughts, drove people away.

We met again in the autumn when she was visiting London
alone. I squired her round the Wallace Collection, to a
French restaurant and a theatre. She was enthusiastic and

appreciative. Over dinner, she declared, 'I am homosexual.'
I nearly tipped my chair over on the flagged floor. 'That
is,' she added, 'I have decided I prefer women to men.'
She insisted on walking hand in hand up the Haymarket.
Glowing, she thanked me for the day, and announced that
she and the children would come and stay at my house, or
rather in her dormobile in the garden, in five weeks' time.

On the train back to my suburb, I realised that this
was the opportunity I had recently become aware of seeking.
In the next few weeks, I knew what those old love songs
were about, all right - 'can't eat, can't sleep, can't
concentrate, I'm losing weight'. My conscience troubled
me, but not too much. My decision was taken, and I was
feverishly in love and so full of anticipation it was
unbearable.

Strange to say, when it happened - late at night,
before the fire in our living room - it was exactly as I
had pictured it and dreamed: thrilling, deeply satisfying,
an intimacy never before reached. 'You feel,' she said,
'as though your heart were being torn out of your chest,
don't you?' Even though Theodora flirted with every man
she saw, Ian's forebodings about getting involved were
fully realised, and our children loathed one another on
sight, I was deliriously happy. Especially when she said,
'Are you sure you've never done this before? Then how do
you know...?'

When they had gone, I told Ian what had happened. Even
if I had wanted to, I couldn't have kept it to myself, but
I had no wish to deceive him. He is brave, strong and
grown-up. He said, 'Good for you.' And 'Well, I wish you
had told me you felt like that before.' And 'Another
woman, I can stand. If it had been another man...' And
'As long as it's as well as, and not instead of.'

They visited us again just after Christmas, against
Ian's wish because he had not liked them. It was a disaster.
My adoration no longer satisfied her. She had overcome
her prejudice against men. She had met Peter, and made a
date with Robert, and was in correspondence with Henry.
But Henry wanted a multiple ménage, Peter had a fiancée
abroad and Robert was drunk and missed their date. Glumly,
in a bitter black frost, we and the children tramped
through the Royal Parks and around the Victoria and Albert
museum. All the time she was cuttingly rude; it is the
way unhappiness takes her. The homesick cats, which she
had brought in the dormobile, messed the dining room carpet
while we were eating a special late-Christmas dinner. The
children - hers, not mine - misbehaved. And, to crown it
all, she demanded her letters - her brilliant and loving
letters - back from me. Cowed and still in love, I gave in.

For a long time, it was as well as, and not instead of.
But I knew now that I couldn't live without a woman to
love. Rushing through a delayed but telescoped adolescence, I cured my heartbreak over Theodora by 'going on
the scene'. A remembered reference set me writing to
Cynthia Reid, the founder of Kenric, one of the earliest
lesbian organisations in Britain, and through her and the

brave and pleasant women in that society I learned the
friendliness and sympathy of the gay world. No hostility
came my way because I was married, no pressure to leave
my family. Only once did someone use the expression
'having the best of both worlds' and that was a young
thing at the Gateways Club. The only pressure on me was
what built up from within, for I came to know gradually
that I couldn't always have it both ways.

At first I went to socials and parties and evenings at
the Gates, dipping my toes in the water. I met some odd
types and some lovely ones. With women I lost the sexual
shyness I had always had with men, though I never did learn
the art of flirting. I had an affair lasting a year and a
half with a married woman - one or two nights a week - but
she ditched me for someone who could live with her when
the opportunity arrived and she was free. When that one
left her, she tried to get me back - the classic fantasy
of the jilted lover. She plied me with gin and food, put
on a romantic record and made a pass at me. 'Sorry, it's
too late,' I said, interested to observe that because my
feeling for her had passed I did not really enjoy my rev-
enge. However, when she threw me over I grieved extrava-
gantly at the time, but I applied the same remedy as
before and went back on the scene. I began to build in my
mind the picture of my ideal: someone warm and loving and
intellectual, who could share at least some of my interests
and put up with my weaknesses.

All this time I hid nothing from Ian. I don't mean I
described the scene in detail to him. He was not especially
interested. But he was aware of what I was doing. For a
time, we were close, Then I began to find it wasn't working in bed any more. I started finding fault with him
about that, but it wasn't his fault he wasn't a woman.
Somehow I didn't feel I had changed, but the more I tried
to explain myself, the less I conveyed. It was just that,
for brief whiles, I found what I really wanted, and it was
worth all the agonising in between. He was sad, but not
bitter.

It was hard getting it across to my teenage children.
They already accepted the fact of homosexuality because
we had gay friends, but how could they associate it with
their mother? Little by little, without dramatic scenes,
they became accustomed to the idea. 'It's your life,'
they said, sighing. 'We always knew you were a bit mad,
Mum.'

I met Tess at a Kenric 'unattached' social. That was
a good evening; there were nice people there, we all
talked a lot and laughed a lot. I was vaguely pursuing L,
L was pursuing A, but it was all lighthearted. A month
later, Tess turned up again and this time she suggested we
go out 'for a jar'.

That was the beginning. I discovered that the hospital
where she worked and resided was not far from where I
lived, and I spent a great deal of time with her when she
was off duty. She was warm and loving, intellectual, and
enormously tolerant of me. By this time I had acquired a

4

car, and that spelt freedom. We drove about in it a good deal. I remember a sudden spontaneous dash to Bexhill to look at the moonlight on the Channel. We went camping; she discovered Suffolk and I discovered the Lake District. We found delight and peace in each other's company. I spent many an illicit night in her confined bed at the nurses' home, and when she went on morning shift I would scrape the frost off my windscreen and return for breakfast with the family.

However, there had to be a snag. Tess was struggling with an existing attachment that caused her a lot of heartache and didn't seem to be leading anywhere. When she qualified, she went away for further training and shared a cottage with her friend, by way of experiment, on the edge of the New Forest. She used to invite me down occasionally for weekends, a strange time of mixed happiness and suffering. She tried, gently, to persuade me that my future did not lie with her. I accused her of using me. It was too sad a scene to be a quarrel. At the same time, it was a situation edged continually with farce.

As I put it to someone at the time: 'A (that's me) loves B. B loves C. C, however, loves D. D loves herself.' Where did we go from there?

I, at any rate, decided to go it alone. I set out to crush my love - that is, my dependence on Tess. It is not easy to crush 'in-loveness' and retain friendship, to cure the disease and leave no crippling after-effects. That is what I tried to do. I went to meetings of Sappho, the London-based lesbian group, and sought new affairs. I tried to satiate desire. Then, on her invitation, I went and met Tess - just as friends, of course - and told her, because she was curious and interested, about these adventures. Tired from my previous night out, I lay down in the cottage to doze. The next thing I knew, she was getting into bed with me.

But I persevered in trying to find a life of my own. I told Ian I must leave him and set up a home somewhere else. I took a full-time job and started to make plans. Tess's ménage with her friend, meanwhile, was breaking up and she was looking for somewhere to live in the area she worked.

At the end of February 1976 there was a National Lesbian Conference in Bristol, and I went to it. A big beery get-together on Friday evening at a club; a march 'to show we exist', routed by the police through back streets where few people saw us (perhaps we were safer there); a noisy and highly political meeting on Saturday afternoon, with no chairperson and consequently complete chaos, those who screamed loudest being those who won; 'workshops' squashed in corners and crammed on cold landings; slogans about wages for housework and wages due lesbians (why on earth?); free ham sandwiches throughout the weekend; a disco on Saturday night at a gay nightclub, the manager and his hefty male staff disgruntled because they were used to gin-drinking men and we women drank mainly beer, so they had to keep heaving barrels up from below; a 'crash' on the floor of the big living room in someone's house, with more

5

and more women arriving throughout the night and squeezing
in like sleeping-bagged sardines; more discussions on Sunday morning, which took place in a draughty marquee because
we had been thrown out of the previous day's mission hall.
It was all a strange mixture of fun and awfulness.

I left them still arguing furiously. The loudest voices
were those from the Left, and they seemed to me to be
speaking, inappropriately, the same heavy language their
big brothers had used when I was at college.

I got home and the family said, 'Tess has been on the
phone for you.' I rang her at the cottage, aware of my new
strength and independence. She had made up her mind. She
thought we could make a go of it. Of course I agreed at
once that we should try, but it was a decision now made in
strength and not in weakness. My days of second adolescence
(' - but you never had a first,' commented my younger
daughter) were over, the disease cured.

The rest is a fairly humdrum story. During the rest of
Tess's training we shared a caravan on a pretty site near
Southampton. I lived at my family home on week nights
while I was working. We settled down pretty easily to
living together - at least, she made a very good job of
concealing her difficulties. After her finals, she agreed
to take a job near London so that I could be within reach
of my work, and we bought a flat in the suburbs near enough
to where my family lived. Two middle-class women on respec-
table incomes, with no encumbrances, we encountered few
obstacles and no rudeness or hostility. My family accepted
Tess as a kind of relative and hers accepted me similarly.
Our lives were enriched by contact with Friends Homosexual
Fellowship, which gave us strength, good friends of both
sexes and an enormous amount of affection - nourishment
everybody needs but not all are fortunate enough to find.

2 Jonathan Fryer

As a kid, I was awfully confused. Ours being a provincial,
middle-class household, sex as such was never mentioned,
but from a very early age (long before puberty) I launched
into a series of mental passions that undoubtedly had a
sexual motivation, even if nothing came of it for rather
a long time.

I first fell in love at the age of eight, with Ingrid
Bergman, in The Inn of the Sixth Happiness. I came out of
the cinema in a swoon, and for months filled my bedroom
with pictures of her, surreptitiously swiped from magazines
in hairdressers'. Not so very many years later, she had
a rival, in the form of David Janssen; I can't remember
when I first would have set eyes on him, but soon he
became a regular feature of my life, as an endless TV
series called The Fugitive brought his great big eyes and
his comforting hairy chest week after week into the living
room.

Cinema seemed far more real to me at that time than

life in Eccles, which had little claim to fame other than
its currant cakes. I was also convinced that film personalities were perfectly attainable, as my elder sister was
going out with one at the time. Soon Ingrid and David
would become aware of my passion, and we would live happily
ever after. So sweet was my delusion that it never struck
me that it was a bit odd that I liked both men and women.
But I did begin to localise the objects of my adoration a
little more sensibly: the girl down the road, the dark-
haired navvy spotted from the top of a bus.

I was nonetheless utterly flabbergasted when something
actually happened. It was on the eve of my seventeenth
birthday, before which I must have assumed that sex (for
now I knew what I wanted, if not quite what to do) would
remain a toy of my ever-fertile imagination. But there
we were, in grimy Salford, with this person making a pass
at me. It was a disaster, but he very charmingly sent me
a birthday telegram the following day.

Unimpressed with this debut, I took to romping across
the Yorkshire moors with a likely lass, also from Salford
(oh, the passion that lurks in and off Coronation Street!),
at which point I shall cut short the litany of my exploits.
Suffice it to say that by the time the next summer came
round, and I had decided to drop everything and everybody
and get on a train to Vietnam to see what I thought about
war, I knew what to do with both sexes, and thought it all
enormous fun.

It was in Saigon that I first became directly involved
with the Society of Friends. And there that I sorted out
my opinions and beliefs about many things, from pacifism
to personal relationships, assisted by subsequent long tra-
vels and meditation across India and the Near East. What
I really wanted, I decided, was a permanent, loving relationship with someone, which would be a marriage of minds
as well as bodies. Sensibly (it now seems to me), I decided
not to predict whether this person would be male or female,
but would leave the options open to see what came along.

However, I must confess that I can't think what came
into my mind on arrival back in Europe, when I checked into
university. At the medical examination, the college doctor
asked me if there was anything I wanted to mention, and I
asked whether he thought it a bit odd that, at nineteen, I
should still fancy some men. I thought he was going to have
an apoplexy. He went bright red, and less than twenty-four
hours later I was seeing a psychiatrist in the local mental
hospital, in a session that one day I should write up for
a film. The central part of the dialogue went something
like:

Psychiatrist: 'What is it that attracts you about men?'

Me: 'People who have beautiful faces. And arms that want
to hold you quietly.'

Psychiatrist: 'Oh, is that all? Well, that's not very
serious. Now, I want you to close your eyes. Think
of a man you like. Now force your mind to turn him

into a girl. Feel her breasts, and...'

He started to get quite carried away with his descrip-
tion of what I should be thinking. I sneaked open my eyes,
and saw that he had closed his. His face bore a beatific
smile as he got deeper and deeper into his own fantasies.
'This man's nuts,' I told myself, 'and to think I'm getting
all this on the National Health!'

I left, and threw myself into a social whirl that usually involved both a boy and a girl at the same time, to
the perplexity and distress of both. The height of compl-
exity was reached when I returned to Asia, settling down
in Tokyo with a boy and a girl who had exactly the same
name. Life became far too complicated.

Then I decided I had to make a choice. It wasn't fair
on either of them, and it was beginning to tear me in two.
The elements of that choice would fill a whole study in
themselves, but I think the most crucial was that the conventional institution of marriage was one that was of no
relevance to me, not least because I had and have no desire
to produce children, and indeed don't even like children
very much. Thus, it seemed to me that a relationship with
a woman would in the end most probably lack an element of
great importance to her; perhaps I would have more to offer
another man.

And thus it is that for the past ten years, my emotional
and physical relationships have been more homo- than heterosexual, though manifesting a pluralism that is both a
reflection of my own make-up and the fact that I am constantly on the move, hopping from one continent to the next,
pouring out books, articles and a stream of correspondence
to a select band of dearly-loved friends and Friends.

What do my fellow Quakers make of this life-style? Certainly I have never felt any resentment or voiced disap-
proval. Perhaps I am fortunate, because I have no skeletons
in the cupboard - for the very simple reason that I have
no cupboard. Thus people have to accept me as I am, or
reject me. For me, one of the greatest qualities of the
Society of Friends is that it is a band of people who
accept, rather than reject; for whom tolerance is not just
a passive attribute but a real desire to understand and to
co-exist. Of course, not everyone in the Society manages
to live in such a generous attitude to their fellow human
beings, but a loving dialogue with the puritanical fuddy-
duddies can open many eyes that one had despaired were
nearly closed.

3

My father died, aged thirty-eight, in the spring of 1906,
leaving my mother with three children (girl of ten, boys
of eight and six), and I was born the following November.
Money was always short, but my mother was thrifty and
always gave to those who were poorer. I had a happy, secure
childhood but was always rather alone. Until my adolescence,

my fantasies were mother/female dominated with a subsidiary black man (perhaps derived from a golliwog). My mother was a devout churchwoman (her faith sustained her through the difficult years of widowhood), later becoming Anglo-Catholic. There was a special relationship with her - I filled the vacuum caused by my father's death after four days' illness, and she wished me to be a priest; but I knew I had no vocation. I was however a choir boy (but I had no voice!) and later became an altar server, absorbed into the Anglo-Catholic tradition, including the sacraments, regular oral confession, and so on. I was disappointed that confirmation caused no physical or other change; the lies told me (in all innocence by a young curate who prepared me for confirmation) about masturbation and the impossible standards of 'sexual purity' that the Church teaching demanded caused deep, unnecessary emotional conflict, anxieties and suffering for the next twelve years or so - it took me longer to forgive the Church for these.

My schooling was minimal, ending with two years' secretarial training. At fifteen I started work in a London local authority where I stayed for forty-four years, being successively promoted - the last twenty-seven years being in a senior executive post.

I became increasingly aware that my inner understanding did not correspond with the religious teaching imposed externally, despite my strenuous efforts to cultivate a 'faith'. My fantasies and unfulfilled sexual desires dominated most of my spare thoughts and energies, resulting in deepening and alarming internal conflicts, and a retreat into myself. I got on well with girls and went to dances with them - they liked my company and I was always a possible husband. I was driven frantic by the urgent sexual drives, relieved by masturbation and looking at muscular men: both manual workers (more fully clothed than today) and physical culture magazines. Above all I visualised a monogamous loving emotional and physical relationship. One isolated experiment with an older man in a swimming pool sickened and shamed me. I felt rejected and isolated, 'an alien to my mother's children', and saw a bleak or no future. I seriously considered killing myself. Thankfully I then met a man, about four years older, when I was twenty-five. David (not his real name) and I became greatly attached, I completely and he partially. Some years later I realised that he was a very devious and complicated person with a bohemian and variegated past and he greatly exploited me, but the relationship enriched me beyond measure, physically, emotionally, mentally and by all kinds of experience, pleasurable and painful, including jealousy, which I managed to negate - most useful.

I knew inwardly that though I was defying the law, Church teaching, and all the current social mores, I was true to myself and my own nature. Eventually I cleaned off my 'false conscience' and inwardly left the Church, though still hypocritically attending and carrying out my various church duties to save distressing my mother.

David was bisexual and extremely attractive to women,

on whose weaknesses he was adept at playing. We discreetly
carried on our relationship under the eyes of family,
friends and office colleagues. He had no regular job.
He eventually had a Civil Defence post. His past leaked
out and in September 1940 he was arrested, became newspaper
headlines, and was deported to America. So ended a ten
years' close, satisfying, but often painful relationship;
but I gained my armour, and a wealth of useful experience,
understanding and self-knowledge.

I had no other gay relationship for the next twenty
years - some of them very grey - but from the end of that
period onwards I had opportunities for one or two occasional
'good times' with older men with whom I had much in common.

My work in London during the war, and my mother's distressing decline, ending in her death in 1946, left me
physically, nervously and emotionally exhausted. I had
other burdens of responsibilities for two friends which
I had voluntarily accepted. I continued to live (and still
do so) with my sister in the family home, and sublimated
my sexual drive into creating beauty in my garden. One
brother died in 1940 and the other married, and died in
the late 1960s.

In 1940 I was under great stress and felt that I could
not continue without any religious belief - I must find
some basic Christian organisation. Quakers seemed to have
the greatest influence for good in relation to their small
numbers, so I went to the local meeting house one Sunday
in November. It was rather damp and musty inside; about a
score of people, all over forty, were there. At the end of
the.hour I felt supported, refreshed, sustained and re-
integrated without apparent effort on my part - something
had been given to me and received. This was a valid experience. I did not understand it, but could not deny its
reality and goodness. I continued to go to meeting Sunday
by Sunday, grateful for its quietness and spiritual, mental,
and physical recuperative powers. (The others present were
detachedly, perhaps too remotely, friendly.) My belief in
the validity of what I inwardly experienced, continuing
from my late teens, was the key which opened the door to
the Society of Friends, in which I continued to develop
and to support within my limitations. I was accepted into
membership nine years later. Moreover, I saw (though many
Friends would not then agree with me) that there was no
incongruity between my acceptance of the rightness of my
gay nature (and unfulfilled longing for a loving relationship with a man) and the Quaker faith.

I later saw that the sublimation of the sexual drive
into gardening was causing a serious imbalance (a 'perversion') in my life. I looked for a way of becoming
heterosexual, which I longed to be, and hoped that this
would occur on my mother's death; but it did not. I tried
alternative 'psychological' techniques. One, the Gurdjieff
'work', was most useful and absorbing, bringing me into
contact with many life 'seekers', including some Friends.
Through it I learned to 'know myself', an interesting,
necessary and humbling task, which rid me of many false

notions of my own 'goodness' and enabled me to verify my
own experiences and to be on my guard about the vagaries
of my imagination. Like the prodigal son, I 'came to myself'. The Gurdjieff 'work' helped me a great deal in other
ways, especially in my job. Through it I achieved a detach-
ment from gardening (which I still enjoy) and a more balanced life.

My life really began on my retirement at sixty, though
the craving for a close, enjoyable, enriching emotional and
physical relationship persists. It is difficult to find
the right man of sixty-plus, especially as I am not 'out'
publicly, and need discretion in view of my home and local
situation.

After a little trepidation, I came into FHF about four
years ago. Words do not describe adequately the open,
loving care, affection, and cheerful air of freedom and
acceptance of its gatherings; and the knowledge that the
Fellowship is always there, rich, full and supportive,
gives confidence to me - an enormous blessing. I have grown
in strength, understanding, sympathy, love and vitality
(and perhaps a little in courage), all caught infectiously
from these qualities shown by its members in so many div-
erse ways. I have yet to 'come out', being hindered by the
complications and perhaps grief it might cause to those
close to me, but this process may occur when the time is
ripe.

4 Peter Martin

I was born in 1943 in Portsmouth. The bombs which terrori-
sed my parents have been replaced in my life by a threat
and a promise far more poignant and dangerous. To live my
life as a gay man, and to celebrate, at the same time, my
fatherhood and my profession, demands a toehold balance
which terrifies and enthrals me. This is how it is.

When I was young - very young - I realised that I was
attracted to men. They held a mystery for me well beyond
the fascination of the lipsticked composure I sensed in the
women I knew. At eleven or so I realised that this was not
an acceptable feeling, and so for the next twenty years
and more I placed my lovingness under wraps. I hid, and in
the hiding nearly suffocated my spirit.

Religion seemed to be the answer. Its insistence on
man's sinfulness seemed to fit. At seventeen I was 'con-
verted' at a Billy Graham Relay Service. I sank myself in
Church activities as a welcome relief from my rather unhappy home. Such teaching as the Church gave on sex was limited to the benefits of chastity and sanctified cohabitation
with a woman. The big 'No' was further propounded by the
kindly but venomous liberality of my college life.

I perceived things clearly, I will give myself that. I
knew I was homosexual, but did not like what I saw, and was
not prepared to live what seemed then a dark, secretive
life. I rejected the idea, not only because it seemed un-

wholesome to me, but because I was well aware, in those
days before the 1967 Sexual Reform Act, of the confusion
and ignorance of the majority of the public. I wanted,
after all, to follow the ambition of my heart and become
a schoolteacher.

And so I married. I was honest with my wife and told
her about my sexuality before we were engaged. We believed
that Jesus would make it OK. After all, 'sin' could be
overcome. Wasn't that what the Gospel was all about? And
if we didn't relate well sexually, then agape, Christian
love, would be enough. We had been well taught to denigrate
physical sex in favour of something 'more spiritual', so
our sexuality didn't seem that important.

I married a woman who was, and is, a brave and solid
person, afraid of many things, yet the kind of human people
like to be around. She, like myself, was very naive. Obedient to our teaching, we had no sex before the wedding. What
followed was a nightmare. (How often afterwards I came to
think of premarital sex as a loving gift rather than unlic-
ensed lust!) Yet despite an ever-increasing distaste for
sex, and related distance from one another, we parented two
boys who are wonderful contributions to the human race.

And it was our sons who stood between us and what was
otherwise inevitable: the break-up of our marriage. I knew,
and know, that I loved them more than anything else in the
world. As the paralysis of tension increased, they were
the only people I could relax and feel at ease with in a
world made for others. I used to arrive home late (I was
by now a head teacher) just in time to see them before
bed. As my behaviour became more and more rigid I began
to turn off even to them.

Yet I would not like you to think I had capitulated to
despair without a struggle. I tried to pray, took advice,
kept myself wickedly busy, and tried so hard it felt as if
I were bleeding. But eventually the crisis came: we had
been married nearly ten years. I went away for a month to
think. I stayed for a while in a monastery where for the
first time in thirty-five years someone, when speaking of
homosexuals, said 'we' instead of 'you'. I could have wept.

It was while I was away that I was encouraged to take
a hard look at the things I still did like about myself -
my ability to care, the way I relate to my children, my
honesty and my intuition. It dawned on me slowly that all
these things spring from sexuality. By putting the lid on
my sexuality, I was effectively closing down all that was
worthwhile in my life. In a very real way I had chosen to
cease to live.

But I kept retreating. Surely to live my life 'in the
service of others' was a preferable (and more comfortable)
way than to stand on the edge of acceptance for the rest
of my life? In any case I was probably only being self-
indulgent. But it was somewhere in the midst of this tur-
moil that it became obvious that I could never love, not
really love, until I had learned to love myself a little.
As it was, even my dutiful fathering of my children was
based on a lie.

It seems to me now that if a course of action is really right, it must against all the evidence of feeling be a right one for everyone. So it seemed then, but it became obvious that this decision would have to be made without the support of my wife. Love had nearly died, and she was, understandably, a frightened, confused woman. I remember with gratitude a moment's insight, when I realised one night that she would rather I died or went mad than face the pain of divorce. I knew at that point it was down to me.

Leaving my family is the hardest thing I have done so far. It took me two goes. My wife, brave and reproachful, did the best she could in the face of the inevitable, and did not actively stand in my way. I told our children my-self. I took them to my new room and told them that their mother and I made each other unhappy. (I had resolved to tell them no lies, but no truths either that they were not yet ready to cope with.) One of them cried and I encouraged him to cry more. Still now, against my feelings, I help them to talk about their sense of loss and bewilderment. I know that every tear shed now, every feeling accepted, is a step nearer to their wholeness.

And so I make no attempt to let things seem like they used to be. We occasionally have tea together as a family since that comes naturally, but I have had to find a new way of being a father. I guard against the 'coke and crisps' syndrome of a Saturday dad, and am proud that the three of us have a real and growing relationship. I take joy in them and have hope for our futures.

So being a gay parent is like so much else about being gay. Nothing is received wisdom. Everything has to be thought out from a starting place of zero. There are no models, no patterns, a virgin snowscape. But unnerving though this is, it feels more real than trying to live out the parameters set up by the nuclear family. Some time ago, I found myself writing in my diary 'I am now living as truly as I am able'.

Being real, being alive and being vulnerable again has set me tingling. I decided to hack down systematically the secrecy and self-oppression that I had hedged myself about with. I joined gay organisations, took part in political lobbying of those who have the power to change the way things are for many gay people; and I told my friends and my family who I am. Their reactions were highly varied. In some cases, sadly, it has meant an interval in a very long friendship; in others, an even closer and firmer friendship. My brothers showed the same spread of reaction: one has cut most ties with me, another showed amazed concern, and the third liberal indifference. My mother asked 'Did it come on suddenly?'!

The task of being open and being alive to who I am made me want to tell two of my colleagues. Not surprisingly they were afraid. One of them brought in a newspaper cut-ting telling how a gay man working with children had been sacked on that basis alone. Ill chosen action as it was, I recognised it was her way of caring. Yet I knew I had to stay out of her fear if I were to cope with my own. Not

13

many months ago, I went unmomentously to my employer and told her simply of my gayness. Why? Because the chief fear I believe is the fear of fear. If I am to be the kind of man I want to be, to be able to offer all that I am to those I care about, to stand sometimes beside others who may need me, then I cannot be pursued by a ghost. I chose to tell her the glad news· so that I was taking charge of my own situation. No more do I want to be governed by fear. I do not want to play the victim.

I live in the village where I work and where my young family lives. I enjoy being here, but wonder where the next phase of my life will find me. So I wait, sometimes easily, on the edge of a chasm. The worst this can offer me is the ruin of my children, the loss of a job I am good at, and an eternity of self-doubt. But the chasm has not yet opened to me. And I remind myself that the choice I faced was not between happiness, fulfilment, marriage - and what I have now. It was a choice between starting to live and starting to die. I chose to live.

5 Alison Brown

I suppose, by most standards, I came out with a bang. Really, it was because, at thirty, I was a very naive entrant into the 'gay world'. For the first thirty years of my life, I'd consciously had no idea that I was a lesbian. True, I'd always felt I was different; I'd never really seen myself getting married, and, at the relatively advanced age of twenty-five, I'd deliberately gone out to sleep with a man. At thirty, I'd slept with several men, though I'd never got emotionally involved in any way. I'd gone for a career, research first and then teaching and my excess energy was worked off in a series of sporting and political activities. After five years' teaching, first in a public school and then at a comprehensive, I realised that I was not particularly happy with the life I'd chosen. From the outside, it must have looked good: I owned a house, had no other ties, was on the local Town Council, involved in many local activities. Yet I was very depressed, a fact which I put down mostly to the problems of the educational system and to my not living, ecologically and politically, in a way of which I approved. So in 1975, at the age of twenty-eight, I threw up my teaching post, and my house, and ended up living in a commune in Shropshire. Here, I thought, I could find a way of life which was both ecologically sound and personally satisfying. And, for a short while, it was indeed so. I recognised that it was in many ways a 'cop-out', but the effort of making such a group work, of living with other people, was an important aspect. I learned a lot about living with others, but I still could not prevent myself from sinking into another really depressed phase. As I had no conscious reason that I could work out, I was desperate enough to seek out a local hypnotherapist. She didn't look for reasons either, but concen-

14

trated on helping me release all the physical tension I'd
held up in my body. With her help, and with the help of
two women in the group who spent a good deal of time and
patience on me, I gradually began to feel that I was sort-
ing out my confused emotional life. Two things came to a
head at about the same time; I realised I should leave the
group to get myself together on my own, and, as I made that
decision, I also realised that I was a lesbian. It's almost
impossible to convey the relief that this understanding
brought. It was a revelation; as though someone had come
along and lifted a ten-ton weight off my shoulders. For
months after that, I was walking on air. The whole of my
previous life fell into place and, for the first time, made
complete sense. I had a sense of the rightness of what I
was doing and felt a complete person for the first time.

In this first flush of my understanding and acceptance
of my sexuality, the problems of 'coming out' didn't really
arise. I was so high myself that it never really occurred
to me that being a lesbian presented problems. We decided
to start a Gay Switchboard in Shrewsbury, which opened -
from the house I was renting - in the first week of December
1977. I'd only left the commune, and realised I was gay, at
the end of August. At Christmas, I keyed myself up to tell
my parents, who live about 150 miles away, and whom I usually see only two or three times a year. I wanted to tell
my mother because she knew something about my previous
unhappiness and discontent, and I felt that she would be
pleased to know that I'd finally sorted out some of my
problems. In the event, she was very accepting, though a
little surprised, and all this added to my sense of security.

The only area where I had not yet been open about my sexuality was at work. In the October, having been on the dole
for a couple of months, I was interviewed for a lecturing
post at a Wolverhampton college of further education. I'd
decided that, in order to earn some money, I should go back
into teaching for a while at least, and, although Wolverhampton is about thirty miles from Shrewsbury, a job in a
college seemed to offer better prospects than one in a
school. I got the job, which started in January. For a time,
work and my life revolving round the gay scene in Shrewsbury
were completely separate. Not being a very sociable person,
and living so far away from the college, I didn't really
have to get involved with my colleagues there after teaching
ended. But,as the months went on and I became used to my
new surroundings and to the students I taught, I began to
feel that it was important to me to be open about my
sexuality.

I think there were two reasons why I wanted to come out
at work. The first was purely selfish: a mixture of bravado
and wanting to be accepted as a complete person in a college
which is still composed largely of traditionalists, among
the staff at any rate. The second was, I like to think,
more altruistic. I knew of no other openly gay people at
college and, counselling on the Switchboard as I did, I was
sure there must be other people there, staff and students,
who were frightened by their sexuality and might welcome

the opportunity to talk to someone who was openly gay. By the summer term I'd decided to make some efforts in that direction.

Actually deciding how to come out as a lesbian was difficult; you can't just go up to a colleague and say, 'Hey, I'm a lesbian!' I decided to start wearing gay badges to work and await results. I was more aware by then of the sort of hatred which can be directed towards gay people; we'd replied to several vicious letters in the press after the Switchboard had started; so it was, in fact, quite difficult. I was very aware of the looks I received and caught myself several times hunching over as though to hide the badge I was wearing. No-one actually said anything to me, but a few days later I got a note from my Head of Department asking me to go and see him. After a few general comments about how I'd settled down in the college, he said he'd had a few complaints about my badges. 'Did I really have to let people know?' he asked. I explained the reasons I'd decided to be open about my sexuality and he seemed to accept it, saying, in fact, that he'd thought I was gay when I came for interview. It was something I hadn't mentioned at the time, simply because my personal life hadn't come up. I still felt that I should be able to wear badges if I wanted to, but I left the matter there until the autumn term, realising that most people now knew that I was a lesbian. Word did travel round: I had a talk with one of the students about it a week or so later.

During the autumn term, a 'Gays in Education' conference was to be held in Birmingham and I decided that I should put a poster to advertise this on the notice-board in the staff-room where information about conferences and courses was displayed. After a day, the notice was ripped down, but there was, of course, no indication as to who had done this. I replaced it. This happened several times, until, angered by this rather childish behaviour, I put a note on the bottom of my sixth or seventh copy, saying that I hoped whoever was responsible would have the courage to come and confront me. The result was that a vitriolic article about lesbians, written by Jean Rook in the Daily Express, was pinned up on the board with various passages underlined. One part I remember was some comment to the effect that, in a lesbian couple, one 'mysteriously becomes the man at bed-time'. Being myself at the time in a very equal relationship which lasted for two and a half years, I was particularly angered at the total lack of understanding, not only from Jean Rook, but also from the people who had chosen to display this example of intolerant prejudice. Rather than tear it down, however (which was my immediate reaction and one which would have lowered me to their level), I wrote a fairly lengthy reply, pointing out not only the ignorance and intolerance involved but also the cowardice of those who could not even confront me with their fears and hatreds. Could they not come to terms with their own sexuality? I asked. As a result my Head of Department again sent for me. He accused me, though in rather an amused way, of 'missionary zeal' but I think he secretly approved of

16

my reply, for I gathered that he'd told the various people who complained that my personal life was nothing to do with my teaching, with which he was quite satisfied.

I still have no idea who the members of staff were who put up the article and there are quite a few people who do not speak to me - nor I to them. But there are also many others with whom I have good working and personal relations and in the last year, at the request of several lecturers, I've talked to quite a few groups of students about the problems and consequences of being gay. As a teacher, I've obviously been luckier than others who have come out and lost their jobs as a result, but I'm pleased that the people I work with are aware of my sexuality - even though some of them use it to dismiss my views - 'Oh, it's her again; she's a lesbian anyway.' It's an odd feeling that there are people I work with who obviously hate what they think I stand for, but I can live with that. At least I'm being honest about what I am and how I feel without hiding parts of it which are vital to my being a complete person. Being a lesbian is a part of me, it permeates my life at all levels; as a feminist, as a teacher, as a person. Hiding it, or even lying about it, as I've seen some of my friends do, just increases the barriers between me and the world and compounds the ignorance and prejudice which does exist.

Coming out is, however, very much an individual affair. For me, I have to be out as much as I can, so I can live the way I want to. Work is one small part of my life, but much more important in many ways is my involvement with the Switchboard, and with our local women's group. Work enables me to afford the house and large garden which I now have, and to live the way I want to, and being out at work means that I'm no longer involved in half-truths and evasions. I can save my energies for being with other people in the gay and women's movements. Maybe if I'd thought more about coming out before I took the plunge, I would have been more cautious and found it more difficult. As it is, I'm happy with the way things have worked out.

6 Noel Glynn

When I met Ted we became lovers, gradually. Attraction was there from the start, sexual attraction, exciting, and sexual pleasure. That is common enough. For me it deepened gradually; friendship and affection grew with understanding until 'I love you' became fitting and right.

In the past there had been years of sexual repression. Years of living with people who appeared to be unaware of sexuality, their own or anyone else's. Years of pretending that sex did not exist, it seemed, so English, so 'cultured'. They acknowledged love, thank God. It was hard to express emotions: I had lost the ability to cry with childhood; it was 'unmanly'. There were years of trying to deny my sexuality. Then when I on occasions allowed myself to admit it, horror, shame that it was something regarded as a dirty

17

perversion.

I could not really be a queer, could I? Where was my limp wrist? Why did I have no desire to molest little boys in the park, or run around in women's clothing? Then why, oh why, were some men so attractive, so exciting? What ever did the other boys see in girls? What on earth was all the fuss about? The company of a girl could be pleasant enough in the right circumstances, but frightening in circumstances where she might expect me to do something sexual, in which I had no interest.

Literature was no help. I read of awful stereotyped 'queers', objects of derision, pathetic characters, bitchy, mentally unbalanced, sick, criminal almost by definition, at best to be pitied, sad and lonely. Could this really be me? No, a book by a psychiatrist gave me hope. It is just an adolescent phase, it assured me, I would grow out of it. Adolescence had come to me late, anyway, so there was still a chance I was going to be 'all right'.

So there were years of relationships with women. They nourished my ego, gave me status, 'made a man of me'. But there was always something wrong, something false at the very core of the relationship. I was trying to force myself into the heterosexual pattern. By my late twenties I had to admit that I was simply the wrong shape to fit that mould. I had to stop being frightened of my strongest desires, find another way to live. There must be no more disappointed women, no more relationships enjoyed for a short time and then cut short by my anguished withdrawal. I am eternally thankful to some of those women. They showed me that a genuine and sincere lover is not possessive, but realistic, and can let the loved one go without bitterness or rancour, even though there is much sorrow.

I started to tell myself I must not feel guilty about being the way I am, for I realised now that I had no choice in the matter. I was a homosexual. I could talk about it with other homosexuals I knew, but they seemed as confused as I was, or worse, bitter. The gay scene in Portsmouth in the late 1960s, what little there was of it, was nowhere to find comfort. I told a few close heterosexual friends. Their support helped a bit, but they could not understand in the way that someone who has had a similar experience can.

Finally, after exploring the gay scene more widely in England and Germany, and not much liking what I found, I moved to London. It was 1971. I was recovering from a bitter disappointment in love. It felt like a bereavement. But in London much was happening to renew my interest in life.

Flower power was still very much in bloom and was growing in the gay community in a big way. Gay Liberation had come to London and was exploding with a tremendous outburst of energy. The message was, 'Stop hiding away.' 'Come out of the closets.' 'Be proud of what you are.' 'Tell the world about it.' 'Fight for your right to be your true self.' 'End the public's ignorance.' 'Learn to love yourself and your fellow gays.'

There was tremendous optimism, a babel of idealism ranging from the sober to the zany; this was the beginning of a new age, an era of peace and love. Revolution was being talked, written and sung about, a gentle loving revolution.

Though retaining a certain scepticism, I got caught up in the general euphoria. I became involved with the Gay Liberation Front and joined the first 'commune' to grow out of that movement. In it I met Ted and started living with him.

It was a very loving community. That quality held it together for over two years until we grew out of it. We certainly had our differences. We encompassed several nationalities, a variety of backgrounds and both sexes. There was a ferment of ideas, revolutionary and reformist, feminist, anarchist, socialist and liberal. We experimented with drag, with make-up, with dance. We organised and demonstrated for our gay rights.

In retrospect I feel that its greatest value lay in our learning what it meant to be gay. I think it changed us all profoundly. Naive expectations had to be modified. No, we could not all love each other equally as some had hoped. Relationships between certain couples deepened and became more fulfilling while not precluding those same couples from enjoying loving and/or sexual relationships with third parties. Sexual jealousy is a real problem, I learned. You cannot enjoy an open non-possessive relationship and expect never to experience it. Monogamous relationships were frowned on, but could any of the alternatives work?

There was no reason why we should assume that monogamous relationships were best for gay people. They appeared to me to be a heterosexual norm devised for the benefit of rearing children in a particular kind of society, in which men control the bulk of the wealth and therefore take the major decisions. They need to know who their sons are so they can pass on their name and inheritance. Women must therefore have only one man, though the same monogamous rule need not be applied so rigidly to men. If the name and inheritance were passed from mother to daughter, on the other hand, there would not be the same need for monogamy, since no woman is ever in doubt as to who her children are. But gay relationships have nothing to do with reproduction and inheritance. At their best they encompass love, understanding, companionship, friendship and eros.

After ten years together with Ted my experience is that if you really love someone you want them to be free. When you are very sure of each other's love, jealousy is no longer the same problem. But there must be complete honesty if trust is to be maintained. No deceit can be countenanced. All relationships must be admitted and discussed. No third party must be deceived either. All relationships need to be approached with complete openness in a spirit of caring.

While living in the commune an event occurred which profoundly changed my outlook on life. I decided to take acid, the drug LSD. It was about; people I knew who had taken it told me it was a good experience, non-addictive and profoundly important in the changes taking place in society. Reading about it had not made much sense to me. It seemed

as though it had to be experienced to be understood. I was
warned that I would probably never be quite the same again,
but that might be no bad thing. I took it. Words are inadequate to describe the experience. Timothy Leary, Damaris
Parker-Rhodes in her Swarthmore Lecture and Aldous Huxley
in his Island and The Doors of Perception have made attempts
to describe the mystical experience induced by psychedelic
drugs.

I felt in touch with a part of myself which exists outside time, with a reality so real that by comparison my
waking life is merely a dream. I felt in touch with a loving force which is so great that it dispels the fear of
death. My love for Ted and his love for me I was shown to
be very special; they seemed fragments of that infinitely
greater love which exists outside time. Though I know it
sounds hackneyed I felt we were intended for each other and
that one of our main tasks in life was to find and recognise
each other. With this revelation lingering doubts about
the rightness of conducting a homosexual relationship van-
ished, seemed absurd.

I felt that as a homosexual I had many opportunities
which were not open to most people. I am free from the
responsibilities of bringing up a family. That gives me the
opportunity of doing plenty of other things.

I felt convinced that as a tiny fragment of the whole
universe I was part of a great evolving mind which is both
intelligent and loving. Just as each of my brain cells has
its part to play in the totality of my brain, so do I and
every one of us have our parts to play in the great mind in
which we are but minor cells. I remember this being so con-
vincing that even my natural scepticism which says, 'This
must be wishful thinking' was convinced.

The scepticism returned after the trip, but my eyes had
been opened to a completely new way of looking at things.
I kept chewing it over in my mind almost obsessively.
'This intelligent loving mind of which I am a part, of
which we are all parts, must be what is meant by "God",'
I concluded. 'It's not a bit like a greybearded old man
sitting on a cloud. Have I gone crazy? I used to be so rational and sceptical - now I'm starting to "have visions" and
"see God". People will think I'm round the twist.'

One morning, in that moment between sleeping and con-
sciousness when one's dreams are accessible to the conscious
mind, I was asking desperately, 'What does it all mean?' A
gentle reassuring voice replied, 'It means you're a Friend,
that's all.' I knew that that word 'Friend' meant more than
simply 'friend', although it included the latter meaning.
I knew that 'Friend' meant 'Quaker'. At the time I knew
little about the Society of Friends, only that they had
some rather unorthodox views about religion and peace, but
I decided to explore my local Quaker meeting.

With my Gay Liberation Front badge defiantly pinned to
my pullover I attended my first meeting for worship. It
was at Muswell Hill. In the silence and with the ministry,
although it was a totally new experience, I felt at home
immediately. I saw it as a tuning in to the wisdom of the

20

loving intelligence of which all beings are but a part. I thrilled at the experience. It was a group meditation in which people spoke with the sincerity of their most deeply held beliefs.

I found I was made welcome among people with whom I could explore the realities glimpsed in the extraordinary vision I had had. I found that they too held in their different ways a vision of part of the same reality. It was often a rather different part, but our fields of vision would considerably overlap.

I had worn my Gay Liberation Front badge because I felt it was important that if I were going to face rejection from the Quakers I should find out about it from the outset. To my great relief I encountered no hostility, not even condescension. I found curiosity and, when I explained what it was all about, a certain embarrassment among some Friends. I felt embarrassed at embarrassing them. I wanted to rescue people from getting embarrassed at me by standing sideways on while talking to them so that they wouldn't be able to read the badge on my chest. It was a real situation comedy. I had to keep remembering that if everyone steps back into the closet the moment they encounter any embarrassment, let alone opposition, gay people will never make any progress in the fields of human rights and self-esteem. We could so easily find ourselves going backwards towards persecution rather than onward towards emancipation.

I kept doubting this new view of reality. I kept feeling that I might be crazy. Well, if I was an awful lot of other people were crazy in the same way. I started to look round at other religious groups and found that when one stripped away all the obscuring clutter of tradition they too held different yet complementary visions of the reality. Hindus, Buddhists, Jews, Muslims, all seemed to be describing the same reality but perceiving different parts of it and using different terms, interpreting it for different cultures.

I learnt that the mystical experience occurs among all peoples, in all cultures and at all times. It can be reached by many other means than drugs and indeed the drug that might induce it in one person would in all probability have no such effect on many others. It is essentially the same experience, however caused, for everyone. It is like being taken as a child for a plane trip over the town in which one lives. Entirely new connections are made in the same reality. When these experiences are interpreted the mystic has to use the language of her/his own culture. Because language is inadequate it distorts the reality and gives it a cultural stamp, be it Christian, Buddhist or· whatever. This discovery served to renew my faith that what I had caught a glimpse of was real.

I returned to the Society of Friends. My vision had nowhere dealt with the figure of Jesus. Weren't Quakers supposed to be Christians and weren't Christians supposed to believe that Jesus is the 'Son of God'? If I hadn't been drawn to Quakers by an experience of Jesus could I really belong there? It took me then seven years to decide that I could and to take out membership of the Society of Friends. Some Quakers, it seemed, like me, did not call themselves Christians but the vast majority did. And a majority among these, when they identified with the word 'Christian', did not mean that they believed Jesus to be a unique incarnation of God, nor that a simple act of faith in him would solve all problems and open the gates to heaven. As I understand it they believe rather that Jesus' teachings are a superb guide to life and that his life and the way in which he met his death are supreme examples of how to live.

I cannot take exception to that, nor could I feel ashamed of belonging to a society that subscribed to that outlook. I certainly could not go along with all the interpretation there is of Jesus' message. I am sure that like Barnabas I would quarrel with Paul (Acts 15: 36-41). There are members of the Society, I believe, who are disturbed that it admits to membership sceptical agnostics such as myself. But no one that I have ever known in the Society has ever expressed such reservations to me direct.

Throughout all my adult life I have had the feeling that humankind is approaching an acute crisis in its social evolution. The two years-odd that I spent working for the United Nations Association sharpened my awareness of the problem. We are destroying ourselves in several different ways. In a world which has enough to feed itself two-thirds are undernourished or literally starving to death, while a minority live in luxury and waste what they have. Enormous resources of human labour and ingenuity are engaged in producing weapons of mass destruction. On a massive scale we progressively pollute the air we breathe and the land and water we depend on for food. Working towards the solution of these problems in one way or another has given my life meaning.

There is a new age way of doing things, that of synthesis. Though religion and science were at loggerheads they are now approaching each other. Westerners are now learning the tolerance and universalism of the East, while Orientals absorb the scientific knowledge of the West.

In the political field too there is a tremendous coming together of different strands. The ecological and alternative technology movement is coming together with the movement for social justice through redistribution of wealth, workers' control and industrial democracy, a merging of the red and the green.

After leaving my work with the United Nations Association, I became involved with a grouping which attempted to embody this political synthesis and give it a little extra momentum, the Alternative Socialist movement. It was another great learning experience for me. We all had different political backgrounds: peace movement, Liberal Party, Communist Party, women's movement etc, and therefore spoke different jargons. Frequently the difference of language would blind us to what was being said. A particular phrase beloved in one tradition could be anathema in another. But at our most profound moments we would cut through these barriers and find understanding. In politics as in religion

I learned that at our deepest levels we are closest. It is here that we more readily understand and love one another.

It is in the Alternative Socialist movement that I gained my deepest insights into the women's movement, although I had learned much about feminism initially within the Gay Liberation Front. I had initially been extremely resistant to what many of the women in GLF were saying. I was inclined to dismiss the more radical women as merely hysterical. I closed my ears to suggestions that as a male I was privileged. But eventually the messages began to penetrate my prejudices. I had to admit that I could walk through our cities at night without an escort and without fear. I had to concede that, despite all the exceptions to the rule I was so fond of, in the main the fact that the majority of the world's wealth is owned and controlled by men gives them the power to take the major decisions in society, business, government, law and their own families. That does not mean that women have no power, or that their power is not growing, or that there are not a few immensely powerful women. I had to admit too that even the structure of most languages reveals the fact that men take precedence: mankind, chairman, the brotherhood of man, l'homme embrasse la femme, God the Father, manpower, management, manhole, manhunt, manslaughter and so on.

When I became involved with alternative socialism, I found that within this grouping the influence of the women's movement was tremendously powerful if not central. Some of the women involved had been researching into archeological and historical evidence for the existence in earlier times of matriarchal societies, or societies of which the organisation was centred on the mothers and their homes. Whilst keeping an open mind on this, largely because I would need to research it myself much more deeply, I grew to feel that the existence of such societies at one time was more likely than not. One characteristic of them would have been that they worshipped the Mother Goddess figure, just as patriarchal societies worship the Father God. People tend to personify God as the most powerful being they can conceive of. In a patriarchy such as ours the female aspects of God have been almost totally stamped out. We are left with relics such as Mother Nature and the Virgin Mary. The latter is clearly obedient to the Father and the Son, even to the point of thankfully accepting a pregnancy she did not ask for and was not consulted about, in circumstances which would certainly have sullied her reputation.

There are however many very beautiful representations of the Goddess in sculpture, preserved from prehistoric times. Traditional archaeologists tend to dismiss them as fertility cult features, but the view that in fact they are the Goddess is gaining ground. All that I can say here is that having once been in contact with these theories the way in which I perceive the universe has taken another significant shift. The patriarchal language which is used even within the Society of Friends is often irritating to me.

A group of us used to meet in London to examine what we

meant by alternative socialism. This was not too difficult
a task except for the feminist aspects of it. We were generally agreed that we would like to see society move toward
a state in which male and female powers were more equal
and in which there was greater understanding and closeness
between the sexes, but how to move towards it was most
controversial. By examining ourselves, using at times various techniques of modern therapy, we kept discovering
more and more differences between the sexes in attitudes
and behaviour. Such differences we felt had their origins
in early childhood conditioning, and in some cases in bio-
logical differentiation. We found at deep levels in our
psyches mutual suspicion, fear and even contempt between
the sexes. Although as a gay man I found that women were
less inclined to view me as a potential threat than they
were the heterosexual men in the group, the implications
of the insights we felt we had gained were that both the
men and the women needed to go through a tremendous amount
of personal change and growth. For example, as a man I
needed to develop the nurturing, caring and intuitive part
of my personality, while the women needed to develop the
assertive and decisive side of theirs. We thought this process of slowly becoming more balanced personalities, a
gradual shaking off of our patriarchal conditioning, would
probably continue for the rest of our lives.

I find there is tremendous resistance to this approach,
particularly among heterosexual men, as the status quo is
comfortable for most of them. But the traditional norm is
uncomfortable for gay men just as it is for feminist women.
It seems to me, therefore, that gay men could be in the
forefront of explaining to the male sex what feminism is
about, an essential step if society as a whole is to move
from machismo to mutuality.

My experiences have given me much to be thankful for. I
am constantly made to feel that the world looks very different to those around me. But I find that more and more
people are looking at it in these same new ways and are
developing new lifestyles accordingly. This gives me great
comfort and hope that although we may appear to be on the
brink of destruction, in fact, so long as we work hard for
positive change, everything will work out according to
divine plan.

7 Hugh Pyper

I cannot remember a time when I didn't find men interesting.
At the age of four I got great pleasure from climbing up -
most insistently - into the lap of a young man who had
come to visit us. He never came back. At school, too, I
was always interested in the other boys (it was a single-
sex school). 'Interested' is the best word, as I cannot
put my finger on the precise fascination. It was akin to,
yet more than, an aesthetic feeling. Somehow the build or
carriage or smile of some innocent youth would hit me in

the solar plexus, just as a shift of harmony in music may twist something inside me. I couldn't think of anything better than to be cradled in the arms of one of these demigods. Actually, at the ripe old age of twenty-six, I still can't.

When a more overtly sexual awareness hit me I'm not quite sure, but it was certainly precocious and rather depressing. I knew that these thoughts were impure and, as a very churchy Presbyterian child, I was early filled with guilt. Indeed, from the age of eleven or twelve I was unwillingly but sanctimoniously resigned to a life of chastity. That did not stop me from being curious or from becoming smitten by someone with great regularity, but, apart from a few awkward adolescent incidents, I remained aloof and sank deeper into a pit of self-loathing.

I was a horribly difficult adolescent, given to ferocious and unpredictable rages, mainly directed at my father though deflected onto others, particularly my longsuffering younger brother. This was at least in part due to my self-loathing which interpreted my father's awkwardness in relationships and equally hot temper as a confirmation of my loathsomeness. It was not a happy time.

I was not totally indifferent to girls, but I knew where my true orientation lay. This made the period from fifteen to sixteen especially trying as everyone else was experimenting with girlfriends and boyfriends and I had neither the interest nor the confidence to follow suit. It was not entirely for lack of opportunity, either. My relationships with boys of my own age were also unsatisfactory. For one thing I was the archetypal sissy, given to poetry and music and with a morbid fear of and physical incompetence in any kind of sport. More importantly, though, I could not entirely trust myself in such relationships. What if I gave myself away?

My attitude to my sexuality was evolving, however. From seeing it as a cancerous flaw in my whole personality, I began to be a little more charitable to myself. Perhaps God had made me unable to take part in the normal traffic of human relationships so that I could dedicate myself to His service. This notion was only a cold comfort as I had come to realise by the age of sixteen or seventeen that our capacity for relationship is the most precious element in our humanity and I was flawed in this, unable to love. My self-esteem was not greatly enhanced.

This feeling did not last. As I left school and went to university, still living at home, I began to acknowledge that I had not been deprived of the capacity for love, but that that love was directed to people of my own sex. I was still developing hopeless crushes on people and, try as I might, I had in the end to admit that these all had males for their object. It was increasingly borne in upon me that no loving God could mean a creature to live an isolated, enclosed life when he had a capacity for love, and, eventually, this became extended to physical love. Not that I would have dared do anything about it! I still had Blake's picture of Michael binding Satan over my bed

25

to remind me to repress myself.

By the time I left university, things had come to a
pretty intolerable pitch. I had taken to driving round
Edinburgh in circles, trying to catch a glimpse of one or
two friends whom I felt particularly close to, but never
daring to admit my feelings. So, when I left home at last,
I was determined to find a man.

And within three weeks, I had. I had gone to Reading to
do a further degree in agricultural botany and as soon as
I arrived in Reading, I fell head over heels for someone
in the same department. To my utter joy, my interest was
reciprocated and after a lot of sighing and speaking sil-
ences, I at last kissed him on the nose. That was it. It
was only the beginning of our troubles, as we had to keep
our relationship completely hidden from anyone else. Also,
my own problems led me to adopt a terribly demanding attitude, and to cause tremendous scenes all due to insecurity
brought on by my low self-image. This proved too much,
things cooled, and one fateful day I went round and said I
thought that perhaps our love was dying. 'That's life,'
said he, quite equably. From that dates the worst year of
my life. First of all, we had to maintain the same relations
outwardly. Secondly, who was I to talk to? None of my
friends knew my secret and most of our friends in Reading
were mutual so I would be letting the cat out of the bag
about him. Thirdly, my own conviction of my unlovableness
was completely vindicated. On top of this, my academic work
was going to the dogs, and the one thing on which I had
built my self-esteem, my academic ability, seemed called
in question. It was all a bit much.

Why do I tell all this? Well, mainly to show how my own
apprehension of the common view of homosexuality had inevi-
tably brought me to a place where I hated myself and had
poisoned all my relationships with deceit and self-defence.
I certainly came close to suicide. What saved me was a
sense of humour and, somewhere, a faith that had outlasted
all my religious doubts. In childhood I had had one or two
ecstatic experiences, a mystical awareness of unity in the
world brought about by an underlying timeless love, and
even in my darkest moods, the light of those moments was
not entirely quenched. With a thirst for truth, I had thrown
over all the preconceived ideas that had been given to me
but I could not in honesty deny those moments, nor escape
the power of the revelation of the Bible. This was the
groundwork I was left with. The humour came in because,
ultimately, I could not take myself so seriously. I knew
that if I committed suicide, I would die a second time of
curiosity, wanting to know what everyone would do afterwards.

Well, how was I to rebuild myself? At great cost to my
pride, I went to a university counsellor. She helped me by
telling me her troubles. I went to a psychiatrist who told
me I was quite right to be depressed and it was nothing
pathological, which was a rather backhanded reassurance.
I began to explore the idea of joining a gay group, though
somehow the idea of homosexuals revolted me. This may
sound strange, but it's true. I had also begun attending

Quaker meetings in Reading, having discovered by reading round that Quakers had the same approach to many subjects as I had myself. I also made up my mind to tell some friends and found that the panic which came upon me was quite unfounded. One mutual friend in particular was of great comfort. This of course meant that I did have to betray my erstwhile lover, but things were at such a pitch that it was inevitable and in the end he was grateful for another listening ear as well.

I also began to launch out into the Reading gay scene, though in my vulnerable state, I spent a lot of time moping in the dark corners of discos. I also joined the university gay group, but as my friend became the intimate associate of the president and his boyfriend, that was really more painful than helpful.

Through my Quaker connections, however, I got to hear about FHF and in great fear and trembling was put in touch with a local member and then went to a meeting in London. Here at last were people who shared my sexuality, my sense of priorities in life and whom I could admire. How liberating it was to find people who were at least in the business of leading what I conceived to be Christian lives without the hypocrisy of denying their sexuality!

Eventually, I decided that I must leave Reading as I was not coping with all the pressures on me. I took refuge in Woodbrooke, the Quaker college in Birmingham. I shall never cease to be grateful for the caring atmosphere where I was able to shed several layers of fear and doubt. One person in particular helped me by his love, though he was not gay, to accept myself as a lovable person in a way that I had never been able to do before. So many people were instrumental in helping me regain a proper self-love, which is so much more removed from egotism than self-hatred.

One major trauma was still to come. My parents had noticed my distress and were obviously due an explanation of my move from Reading. Resolving that half the truth is worse than none, I wrote them a letter containing much of what I have said here, and then waited. Of course, the post was delayed, but their answer, and their subsequent behaviour, surpassed my wildest hopes. Strangely, my relationship with my father became much less strained as a result, which is a great testimonial to him.

Since that time, I have never again, thank God, sunk to those depths, though my self-confidence is not quite as rock-founded as I like to imagine. Today, I accept my homosexuality gladly, without guilt, and perhaps even thankful for the insights I have gained through my struggles. In some ways, it is still a handicap. As a teacher, I am chary about letting it be known at school as my job might be in danger - a compromise with hypocrisy, as I don't see myself as any more of a danger than my colleagues in a mixed-sex school. There are still some friends I have not told, afraid of their censure, though this becomes easier and easier. Generally, though, I have been incredibly lucky in my friends, and perhaps some of the most important relationships in my life are with straight male friends. It is

a joy to be a channel whereby another male can explore his
feelings of tenderness without being constrained by the
sexual role expected of him in a normal heterosexual relationship or with his peers. 'Glad to be gay?' - well, perhaps more 'Glad to be', though not without times of doubt
and despair, but I am glad that, in at least one region of
life, the house of my personality has been blown off the
sands of convention, and has had to be rebuilt, a little
more firmly founded on the rock, I trust.

Many people, however, are stuck with a terrible concep-
tion of themselves, reinforced by stereotypes seen in the
media and by the unthinking reactions of others. It is almost worse for caring people who see their worth in the
quality of their personality and relationships rather than
in wealth, strength or power. It takes great courage to
maintain one's inner balance against the world's opprobrium,
but I know how damaging the imbalance can be and the trans-
forming effect of seeing the power of love and honest working together. There are many forces in society which prefer
a deceitful unity to an honest diversity, and many fears
which are bred from deceit. Fear breeds deceit in my own
life still, which is a sorrow and a sign of cowardice. If,
however, we can be patient with each other's deceit, perhaps
we may all grow in honesty, and thus in truth.

8 Martina Weitsch

Once, when I was about twelve, we had a weekend Quaker
gathering in the town I lived in, and therefore a few
Friends staying in our flat. Conditions were crowded, which
meant that I had to share a room with my sister and another
Young Friend, Anna, who were both fourteen. I admired Anna
very much - she was one of my many crushes. That evening
she and my sister were talking about boys they liked and
the sort of relationships they wanted with boys. At some
point my sister said that if only she had a 'boyfriend',
life would be just fine. I said that I'd settle for a girlfriend, implying that girlfriends weren't either as valuable
or as important as boyfriends. They both sort of laughed
and probably thought that I was just too young to know. But
I knew quite consciously even at the time that I really did
want and would have preferred a girlfriend, not only because
even then I knew I was a lesbian, but because I was desperately lonely. Young lesbians in those days (1965) did not
have many friends.

What I was looking for was neither the other girls with
whom talking was chatter about boys and clothes, nor the
few girls and women I had crushes on and admired so much I
never knew how to talk to them. I was looking for a real
friend - someone who shared my experience and my thoughts,
my feelings even - in short, another young lesbian.

Years later, I found myself in another discussion with
women. I had come out to myself, my family and the 'whole
world', and I had joined the women's movement and the fem-

inist publishing collective Frauenoffensive in Munich. We were organising a conference for women writers - professionals and those who 'only' wrote for themselves. I was very involved in that. Stubbornly I insisted on having a separate workshop for lesbians. I had met Barbara once before very briefly and I knew she was interested; I was sure there would be many of us who would find this a welcome opportunity to discuss our own writing in the context of the general lack of lesbian literature and fiction. So I made sure all the lesbians I knew to be closet writers were there.

On the day there were ten of us packed into the smallest of the available rooms. It was difficult to start because we had internalised the opinion that we did not exist in society, and that therefore our contribution to literature could not be important. Of course we knew of the few great exceptions - Sappho, Gertrude Stein, maybe one or two others - but at least they were historical and dead, two points we did not have in our favour. So we tried to start by telling each other what sort of things we wrote and why we wrote and whether we still wrote. I can't remember whether Barbara began, or who spoke before her, but as she told of the many letters she'd written to friends and women she admired, suddenly my own memories came to life. Barbara was telling my herstory.

There were the early crushes on girls which tried to be no more than the usual schoolgirl friendships. I remember specifically one girl, Gabi, who was two years younger than myself. We must have been twelve and fourteen at the time and went to the same school. Endless series of letters from me to her brought with them all the excitement of new love - but hardly any response. We spent a lot of time together - in spite of that - and of course, sooner or later, she noticed that more was happening than just the camaraderie of kids. She was scared, but she never said anything. Then one day she informed me that her father had told her she could not see me any more because my grandmother had been Jewish. Her father had said nothing of the kind; her father knew nothing at all about the whole thing. I knew it and she knew that I knew; but still I had to cope with double rejection: for my background and for my orientation.

The worst part was that I understood the whole process too well - I felt obliged to play the game; I told people who asked - and not many did - that we weren't seeing each other because I was Jewish and her father would not have her mix with Jews. I listened to people's explanations, comfort and reminders that I needed to be patient, and I listened to my mother telling me that I was behaving like a young man 'in love'. I guess she knew more than she would admit, and I guessed it then, but those were the unwritten rules of the game: you didn't say what you really felt or thought.

But crushes come and go and I was never short of a recipient for my never-ending letters. Not all of them my peers either. Ninth grade saw the arrival of a new teacher who made herself unpopular within minutes of the beginning of the first lesson; but she did teach music which was my favourite subject. And anyway, her unpopularity was the best thing that could have happened to me. It made her vulnerable and seemingly put her in a position where she needed protection. Enter the brave knight - minus the white stallion, of course. I defended her all the way; what better way to cover up my own exclusion? Of course she ignored me - unless I was mending her bike. She encouraged my pursuit of musical excellence, and both she and her daughter found it very convenient to have someone with whom to share their woes. They were both sleeping with the same man, both pregnant by him and both telling me in confidence about their abortions.

I worshipped the ground they walked on. My fantasy was that the mother would break down and sink into my arms, only to realise then and there what it was she'd always wanted. Needless to say, it did not happen. But I did spend three years of my adolescence pretending to myself that this was a friendship.

These were two of many platonic affairs, sublimated into letters which are now irretrievable and which tell the story of a lesbian childhood.

Barbara and I had a glorious half-hour finishing each other's sentences, laughing before anyone else knew why, when laughing was the only way to deal with the pain.

This was the friend I'd looked for for so many years. The sadness lies in the near certainty that if we had recognised each other then, the very recognition would have driven us apart in fear. Now we were meeting at the right time; when we needed, more than anything else, the reassurance that our experience was relevant, shared and real. We were both involved in permanent relationships; the present, with its ups and downs, was fine. It was validation of our past that we needed from each other and that was something we could give each other, and wanted to give.

We lived 150 miles apart and both still went to college. So we spent many hours on the phone and wrote many long letters. In a way we were following the patterns of our teenage years; but this time it was on equal terms. This time it was not the constant feeling of one pursuing the other. We knew that we both were dependent on each other in much the same way. There just wasn't anybody else who understood really what a lesbian childhood and adolescence is like. Although the best environment we had ever found for survival was - and still is - the women's movement, there were few other lesbians there then, and none who had been lesbians from such an early age.

Whilst in the movement women were, rightly, condemning patriarchal values and the imitations of men women had been forced to become in order to make it in society, we needed to speak about our jealousy of men, jealousy we had lived with for years. We had fantasised about being men so as to be allowed the love of women. The movement was criticising the 'bar scene' - those semi-secret and expensive clubs, where lesbians can be 'themselves' for a few hours after dusk and before dawn, looking - always - for the love of their lives - because lesbians were being exploited, and exploiting each other; for us the bar scene had been the first place where we met other lesbians, the first place where we belonged, our only home.

Our correspondence enabled us to relive the significance of writing letters, but this time knowing they would be answered. In one of them Barbara wrote: 'I'm glad that you are there. If anybody can understand all this it is you. And I just had to get it all out on paper. Even if it isn't new, even if we know it all: unfortunately we know it all.' During those two years we planned two projects. One was a film about our growing up, the other a book of lesbian art and culture. Neither project ever materialised, partly because of a lack of finance, partly because we spent so much time talking, and we both went through quite considerable upheavals in our other relationships. But I think it was very important for us to discuss these two projects because they have given us the strength to believe in the relevance of our own herstory as lesbian culture. We were able to affirm our strength - which had always been classified as masculine - in new terms: as the strength of lesbian women. But we were also able to share some of the weaknesses, the vulnerability; to confess to each other that sometimes we would grit our teeth and laugh when we'd far rather cry because the comfort we needed was inaccessible. We had both pushed ourselves and been pushed into growing up too soon because we couldn't share important experiences and developments with our peers. And perhaps that is the essence of a lesbian childhood - growing up too soon and too self-sufficient. I think it is no coincidence that we both went to the USA on exchange visits when we were fifteen - to a foreign country with a language we hardly spoke when we got there. It was the biggest challenge of my teenage years, and the only one I could talk about. But even that I could only do in fragments. Out there I was alone, trying desperately to fit in when I didn't on two counts. And coming back - 'home' - nobody knew what it had been like, and nobody wanted to know.

So when Barbara and I were able to share that experience too, it was for the first time - seven years later for me, five for her - that either of us could say that apart from the maturity we had gained from the experience, there was also a painful realisation that we wanted a security and a safety that would never be accessible again. Subsequently I have discovered that many a dyke with a lesbian childhood has that same sense - a wish to be able to go back to childhood.

Barbara and I now live three thousand miles apart, both in foreign lands again, but 'as women' - as lesbians - 'we have no country...our country is the whole world'. We see too little of each other and we don't write all that often now, but the friendship remains. The certainty of this friendship still validates the experience I don't share with many others - still is what sisterhood means to me.

9 Clive Spendlove

I first went to a Quaker meeting for worship in January
1978. My previous religious experience had been a varied
one: childhood attendance at Church of England; witnessing
at the age of ten the results of my mother's conversion to
Roman Catholicism; practising yoga at fifteen, and selling
as many of my possessions as my parents would allow in
order to contribute to Mother Theresa's work with the dying
and destitute. At the age of sixteen I became one of
Jehovah's Witnesses, leaving school in order to do full-
time witnessing work; however, by seventeen I had started
to experience a withering away of my newly-found faith, by
what may have been a combination of an alternative evangel-
ical theology and the great effort required to do the witnessing work in the face of sudden fundamental doubts such
as: 'How do I <u>know</u> for sure that the Bible is true?' and
'Suppose "God" does not exist after all, and I'm telling
people myths?' (Luke 8:13).

Soon I felt unable to continue the witnessing work and,
greatly depressed as I came to be as the meaning to everything crumbled away, I refused to believe anything <u>just</u>
because I wanted to. For four or five years I floundered
about between belief and non-belief about some big religious questions, and even now there is much agnosticism in
me which I find unsatisfying and frustrating after such
one-time certainty. I tried various other forms of worship
after I lost my fundamentalist Christian faith - a faith
based on the Bible. However, during the last couple of
years, not only have I been helped in coming to terms with
my current spiritual position, but also at the same time
I've been experiencing some answers to my questions. Much
of this change I attribute to Quaker worship, and particularly to my experience of this with and through Friends
Homosexual Fellowship.

I now want to write something about another aspect of
my life's searching - which is probably very much connected
to, or even part of, the area of life we usually call
'spiritual' - that is, my sexuality.

Living in a Yorkshire mining village, to be a 'poof' was
The Worst Thing. I can remember the taunts, rejection, and
ostracism from junior school days. I didn't know what those
words meant, and perhaps neither did many of the pupils who
said them. As a child I was very much alone amongst other
children, yet I cannot remember experiencing loneliness
until after I had begun to leave the Jehovah's Witnesses -
probably the first group to which I had felt I belonged,
in which I felt acceptance and love.

As a young boy I think I used to console myself with
food, and consequently became very fat; this, of course,
made me subject to even more ridicule and isolation. And I
was very sensitive. I can remember one of the first days at
school, when I looked around the playground in horror and
fear at the fighting and gang intimidation. Of course I

never fought back, which encouraged them to pick on me all
the more. At first my parents used to try to shame me into
defending myself, but instead I only stopped telling them
about the cruel treatment I was receiving, and my unhappiness expressed itself in other ways including aggression
at any coercion or discipline from my parents, and neurosis.
Anyway, I've never learned to fight: I've been a pacifist
as far back as I can remember.

I hardly ever experienced being part of a team. The
other boys didn't want to know me, so I found some companionship with a few of the girls. I never learned to play
games like football, and by the time I got to grammar school
I was so embarrassed by my almost total incompetence at
sport, and by my massive size, that I managed to get the
doctor to write a permanent excuse note!

I knew virtually nothing about sex until I was around
fourteen: there was no sex education either in school les-
sons or at home. However, looking back, it does not seem
that I wasted much time once I had found out, because I was
having a regular sexual relationship with an eighteen-year-
old girl when I was fifteen. Although the various stages
to our relationship were largely at her instigation, I did
enjoy the experience; however, towards the end I was having
homosexual fantasies, and this squared with the vague feelings I had previously had in certain situations with other
males.

Religion came into my only heterosexual relationship
when one day in school Divinity class I found out what
'fornication' was said to mean. I felt that I had to put
a stop to the sexual part of the relationship, if I was
going to call myself a Christian according to what Jesus
said, because we were not married. Primarily because of
what it said in the Bible, I did not have a sexual experience with another person for the next five-and-a-half
years; towards the end of this period, when my faith was
on the rocks, the reason for my celibacy was - I thought -
because I didn't know how to get a girlfriend.

When I was twenty, I was so lonely that I decided to
have some counselling from a marriage and personal guidance
counsellor. One of the outcomes of this was my contacting
some people whom I knew to be homosexual, in Friend (a gay
counselling and befriending service), and in the Campaign
for Homosexual Equality (a social and political organisation). For a couple of years I was, as with religion,
alternately in doubt and faith, about whether or not I
wanted to be gay, whether or not it was all right to be gay,
and whether or not I was gay.

Eventually, after a couple of years, I decided finally
that I was going to accept my homosexuality (although there
is a smaller degree of heterosexuality in me), that it was
how I was, and that I was going to celebrate it by being
glad to be gay. Also, I decided that it was OK to be gay
because I was being true to myself, and my open and honest
experience had shown me what was right for me. I felt that
I had to reject Christianity, as incompatible and opposed
to what I had realised myself to be. I had tried to 'be

33

heterosexual' but was unable to be rid of the sexual attraction to other men - which previously I had often considered to be 'physical, but not necessarily sexual' in character.

I think I must have seen Friends Homosexual Fellowship advertised in Gay News. There was certainly nothing at the Friends Meeting House about it that I had seen. I made enquiries about FHF, and then travelled from Yorkshire to Manchester for my first FHF North West group meeting, which was held in a private home. I came away from the meeting more confused about the compatibility of homosexuality and Christian teaching, and I could see a similar clash between feminism and the Bible - questions had been discussed such as 'Why should God be only male?' I resolved to have nothing more to do with such tortuous nonsense as Friends Homosexual Fellowship, and I tried to explain by letter to them how misguided they appeared to me.

Some of the members whom I had met that day in Manchester kept in touch with me, and I think it must have been this contact - from two women in particular - that led me to consider attending the FHF Day Conference at Hampstead Meeting House in October 1979.

A few weeks before that conference I had started trying to form a gay group in my West Yorkshire home town, an area which for some people had meant living twenty miles from the nearest meeting place for gay people (a CHE group or a gay disco). That weekend in October 1979 was a break from the almost full-time business I had been putting into the organising, meeting of enquirers, publicity, etc. But the Day Conference was significant for me in my spiritual development, for I had an experience - or, at very least, the start of one - which has been unique for me, and has deeply affected my life since then.

It was after I had returned home that I began to notice a change in myself, which was largely characterised by a feeling of much greater spiritual peace than I had experienced in years. This goes back, I believe, to the period of silent worship with which the Hampstead meeting was ended, when, after what for me was a fairly intense several hours' listening, talking, thinking and meeting Friends, when we had been talking about matters relating to spirituality and sexuality, and also observing and feeling the emotional openness among the people there, there was a communion in the silence, in which I had an extraodinary feeling of what I may describe best as 'having arrived'. I could see that somehow, my life up until that point had been a preparation for the time and place in which I then was, and subsequently would be. It felt like 'knowing where I was in relation to the rest of existence' and I felt I had a new inner guidance about what I had to do. I felt I was truly alive 'here and now'. The words with which I try to describe this experience are probably only my attempt to make sense of what happened, for myself and the reader.

My flat was no longer suitable for the growing group, as up to thirty-five people were attending meetings. I applied to the local Friends Meeting to use their premises, but was refused. The fact that they declined my offer to come

34

and discuss my application and their reasons for refusal
did put me off quite a bit. But I continued to find FHF
meetings more and more helpful and caring. I tried other
Churches - other than Quakers - but I could not last long
in attending their services, because however much I felt
an emotional pull back to the Mass, I just could not believe
much of the Creed, so I didn't enjoy attending because I
felt dishonest in taking part. I do not know of anywhere
else that I can go to, out of all the religious groups I've
ever been in touch with or know anything about; only the
Society of Friends. I have been an agnostic, and an atheist,
and I have made many attempts to believe in what I understood to be 'the Christian faith'; now, through Friends
Homosexual Fellowship, I have been able to hang on to something which embraces both my doubts and beliefs, the
Society of Friends.

Now - a year later - I am starting a North-East group
in FHF, and, to my great joy, I feel ready to become a member of the Society of Friends. It has been through the fellowship with homosexual Friends that I have been able to
stay in touch with the Society of Friends, and which has
now led to my application to join, and which has brought
me the spiritual peace of mind and heart which I doubted
I would ever find, along what often felt like a very solitary path of agonising after truth.

Maybe some or all of us can only find God, Truth, Enlightenment, in the creation of God in which images of God are
to be found and perhaps especially in those humans who
'nurture that of God within them'. Also, I think, how can
we ever hope to find out what is true if we, as seekers
after truth, are not honest - and that applies as much to
sexuality as to anything else.

10

I am a single man, now aged thirty-nine, and a member of
the Society of Friends. I do not disclose my name, out of
consideration for my parents who are still living. Most of
the things in the account that follows are however known
to them, and to a wide circle of friends, within the Society
and elsewhere. I thought it might be of some interest to
describe what can happen when a person with homosexual ten-
dencies comes into the hands of the law.

As long as I remember, I had emotional feelings about
other boys around me. Even as a small child, I was very
moved by the sound of boys singing. When my aunt read tò me
that dreadful verse 'What are little boys made of?' I protested loudly. It seemed to me that there was an adult
conspiracy to put boys down, and say how much better girls
were. I can't actually recall anyone saying that in as many
words, but the feeling was in the air, and at the age of
five I very much resented it.

As a child, my relationship with my father was weak:
with my mother, it was stronger but problematical. She

expected me to be older than I was, and once or twice said
most unwise things, such as when she compared me to two
friends who were both adopted, saying, 'X and Y are both
adopted, but they bring their mothers a lot of happiness;
you're my own child, and you bring me nothing but misery.'
I was too young to understand what 'my own child' meant,
but I was frightened and it was moments like this that
built up in me the feeling that women were somehow unrea-
sonable and impossible to please, and relationships with
them threatening. It was a pity I had no other male relations on close terms; I had a younger brother, a much more
likeable and contented boy, who made me feel jealous. In
later years he became a great ally.

From seven to eleven I attended a strict boys' school;
you were not allowed to go to the lavatory except at pre-
scribed times, and this caused severe difficulties. Sometimes there were fifty boys in a class. I liked the teachers, but I regret now that they, as well as the pupils,
behaved as if females were somehow sub-human; they showed
an open contempt for their colleagues in the girls' school
next door. I was extremely isolated, feeling at times a
conscious barrier that prevented me from joining in games
in the playground. When I was ten I tried to kill myself.
It was a serious attempt, not just a gesture of despair.
While my childhood had many happy episodes, the prevailing
emotional climate was tense and dutiful, rather than happy.
At ten I felt the first stirrings of lust, as a sort of
uneasiness and restlessness; I was preoccupied with the
human body, and developed a strong attachment to a much
smaller boy in the school. I was so in awe of him, I felt
afraid to go near him. I was physically very advanced, and
could ejaculate when I was eleven. I had no instruction on
such things of any kind, though I suppose I knew what was
happening from the talk of other boys who had older brothers.

My IQ at junior school was said to be 150, though I did
not know that at the time and find it hard to believe now.
I won a prize for my performance in the eleven-plus exam,
and then went to a co-ed Quaker boarding school. This gave
me a fresh start, away from the stress of home, but I was
wandering in the emotional complications of adolescence
while others round me were still free and uncomplicated
children. My first two years were particularly dreary, en-
lightened only by new school subjects such as Chemistry and
French, and by a longstanding fascination with railways (it
was the routes and timetables that most interested me, not
the mechanical side). When I was fourteen, I was allowed
to have my bike at school and the headmaster generously
gave me permission to go on country rides alone, which was
against the usual rules. I hardly ever had anyone to go
with me.

As early as my first term at boarding school, I approached both a lady and a man teacher, trying to speak about
the way I felt towards other boys; perhaps I was too diplomatic, but I got the impression they were nonplussed and
certainly unable to give me advice. I was alarmed about
that time to come across the term 'homosexual' and realise

that it applied to me. I was appalled to find that I wanted
to do things which were against the law. I was not delin-
quent in other ways, and never told lies or stole or smoked.
There was no virtue in that, as I was never even tempted
save in this one unmentionable area of life. I had to face
the fact, as young as that, that all sex was regarded as
evil, and because this made me so guilty, I never really
grew past that stage.

I did well at O level, less well at A level, but won a
scholarship to the Cambridge college that was my first
choice. That was a big step to take: noone in my family
had previously had any further education at all, let alone
university, let alone Oxbridge. That period of my life was
however not at all happy. There were my own continued frustrations, coupled with the threat of destruction by the
Bomb. Two books I read as a sixth-former focused my disil-
lusion with the adult world: The Go-Between and Lord of the
Flies.

As a sixth-former I organised activities for the younger
boys in the school, who were a neglected group; that was
one of the more socially useful things I did there. Though
I was closely interested in individual boys at times, I
went about with whole groups and was careful also to get to
know the parents. My classmates were a little amused and
puzzled, but some people in middle school made my life a
misery, trying to point out to the twelve-year-olds what my
supposed motives were. This was hardly fair. It was these
experiences that carried me forward into the first adventure
of my adult life, which was a temporary teaching post in a
boys' secondary modern in a depressed Victorian town. On
the strength of this I decided I would teach as a career,
though it did not seem altogether a wise decision, and I
was always aware that I might move on to something else.
That first post went better than either of the two I held
subsequently; maybe it was beginner's luck, and anyway twenty years ago schools did not attempt the range of activities
they do today, with all the attendant stresses for the
staff who must nowadays devote their whole lives to their
job. But I scored initially because I related so well to
an age group no one else seemed to value: I really did care
for eleven-year-olds, the bright and the stupid, the sturdy
and the pathetic, in shorts and jeans and jerseys; I warmed
to a certain eagerness of response children of that age
used to show, and enjoyed the tension between the lingering
dependence of earlier years, and the new assertiveness of
adolescence. Boys of that age will walk ten miles, climb
rocks, eat voraciously, but still want to be tucked up in
bed or read to until they fall asleep.

At university, I deliberately avoided any sort of activities with boys, to give the whole situation a chance to
sort itself out. I did have a girlfriend during those
years, an attractive person though she didn't share much
in any of my enthusiasms. Our relationship never became
more than companionable, however, and this may explain why
on some occasions she treated me very badly; she wanted
more than I could provide. I proceeded after that to a

postgraduate teaching course, and then taught for thirteen years: first in a remote North Country grammar school, and then for ten years in a comprehensive school in a New Town. I see now that it was not quite honest to have sought no help during college years; I knew very well that anyone I approached would be bound to advise me not to teach. I had heard of teachers coming unstuck over relationships with pupils, and was determined this should not happen to me. And it never did.

However, something else happened in the end. During my teacher training year, I was one of three students selected to care for small groups of children from problem families who were isolated and in need of befriending. This project formed part of the groundwork for a book one of my tutors subsequently wrote. It made much the most interesting part of the course for me, and my relationship with the five boys in my group, then aged ten, grew so strong that I still see three of them now, eighteen years later: they are now married, with children of their own. My relationship with these boys remained manly and positive, though it was achieved in the face of considerable initial struggle: they would accept me, but not each other. However, one belonged to a family even more isolated than the rest; the first thing I knew about him was that his father was serving a prison sentence for a sexual offence against his own daughter. When I was invited to the house, the thing that most impressed me was not the physical squalor of the place, though that was memorable; it was the group of younger brothers, whose need for someone from outside to accept and love them, in their family's disgrace, was so evident that I was bowled over. I started overnight an obsessive involvement with this particular family that lasted many years, and involved a great deal of comedy, much suffering and final disaster.

The mother accepted me warmly from the first; the father's attitude varied, and I entirely sympathise with his feeling that I was in danger of eclipsing his influence over his children by offering them adventures he could not hope to provide. I was very careful to be seen to support the parents' authority; indeed, within the limits of the low mentality that they all shared, they were able to operate as an effective family group for most of the time, and the parents were genuinely concerned for their children's good. There were some violent incidents over the years and I am certain the boys had early sexual experiences, of one sort or another. Their lives tended to be lived very much in physical terms.

As time went by, I reached a kind of impasse in both my personal and my professional life. Though I continued to enjoy warm relationships with many individual colleagues and pupils, I got nowhere near overcoming certain basic difficulties, and I see now that the local stresses operating in the particular community where I spent so long did not help. I lived alone, in an attractive series of homes where friends seemed always glad to come; but the long hours I worked cut me off from the normal range of contacts, and I spent time at weekends and holidays with pupils, organising activities for them because that was the side of my work I was best at, and it compensated for my declining success in the classroon. I expected all the time that sooner or later things would change, and I should acquire a wife and family of my own. I did make some progress; my relationships with my numerous women friends have grown more trusting, and even romantic, but they have never involved sex. My married friends never see me as a threat, but rather as a support to their own relationships. I have been helped immeasurably by this, and it was the support of such people that enabled me to cope as well as I did at the time of greatest trial.

I ask myself why, knowing myself as I did, in the end I broke the law. It was certainly not because I believed the law was wrong; I faced a lot of stress, because in other respects I am conformist, even conservative in outlook. I have always sought commitment in relationships. But there are limits to self-restraint; I had no sexual contacts with anyone at all between sixteen and twenty-eight, the very years when most males are sexually likely to be most active. I knew the younger brothers so well by this time that there were no secrets at all between us, and conversely, the usual constraints that would operate between teenagers and a grown man gradually ceased to apply. I had had a lot of close contact with them as children - there were four by this time - but there came a time when they were too big to sit on my lap, be bathed and dried, or carried on my back when they were tired. But the need for acting out our devotion remained. I do not say this to excuse myself, or flaunt my misdeeds in the face of others through a desire to shock. I am merely stating what happened at the time.

The first occasion when I clearly broke the law was with the oldest of the four younger brothers, who was then sixteen. His older brother and girlfriend were staying at my house at the time, and were sleeping in the other room. The temptation to copy what they were doing (or what we thought they were doing) was more than I could resist. Later I gave this particular boy a temporary home for two periods when he was at loggerheads with his family, but had no job so he could not go into lodgings. I felt extremely guilty about the new stage in our relationship, but this did not stop me from getting involved, over the succeeding years, with the younger three boys when they got to the stage of making sexual approaches to me. They had certainly done similar things with other boys (not, I think, with men) and I would strongly deny that I corrupted them, or made them take part in things they did not want to do. The actual offences consisted not just of 'playing about', but a good deal of affection, close embraces and sharing of emergent maleness. A Samaritan told me, 'The physical involvement is the price you pay for the depth of your concern.' A psychiatrist pointed out that I was not ill, but was bound to be under stress because I wanted so much something that society was not prepared to allow.

Once I had got involved with the youngest of the boys,

then aged eleven though sexually very knowing, I was almost certain to be found out though in the event I was not arrested until a year after that. This happened in a way I should have foreseen and warned the boys about. The most backward two tried out their games on a little cousin who came to stay. He told his mother about it on his return home and she, quite correctly, referred the matter to a social worker for advice. This person, apparently without further thought or consulting the records of the family, called in the police who interviewed the two boys. Not surprisingly, in their distress they turned to the one adult who might have been in a position to support them. But I had returned from a school expedition to the Isle of Wight only the night before, and I felt too tired to face the bus journey of two hours to their house; so I failed to help them. They saw this as desertion in their hour of need, began to talk about me openly, the mother overheard them and sent for the police on her own account. I had a tip-off from the oldest boy that there was a warrant out for my arrest, but in the day that then elapsed, I did none of the things that one is advised to do in such circumstances except for contacting the Samaritans who supplied me with a solicitor. (He proved a worthwhile ally.)

It was fortunate that my arrest happened in the school holidays. My headmaster, himself a JP, came to see me immediately he heard I was in custody. Two of the boys (the oldest now twenty-two) were also arrested and kept in the cells for questioning. All were subjected to gruesome medical examinations which I should have thought amounted to serious sexual assault. Charges against the boys were eventually dropped, but the youngest was taken into care for the four months I was on bail, presumably to prevent me from seeing him. It was a bail condition that I should not try to contact the family, and I observed this punctiliously though it was a very great strain as naturally anyone would want to discuss a difficult situation with the people it most nearly affects.

I was certainly not physically maltreated by the police myself, though I found it hard to take their preoccupation with sex which excluded any other human considerations in the case. I referred when making a statement to the trust and affection which had existed between me and the boys, but the inspector said, 'Leave that out.' My solicitor protested, and this particular remark was put in. But I had some difficulty in persuading some of my friends that the boys had really consented to what had occurred between us. 'If they consented,' they said, 'then why have you got into trouble over it?' Some people are as little informed on the operation of the law as that.

The detective's view was quite clear: he believed homosexual acts were wrong, and he was out to suppress them. He questioned the boys endlessly about their relations with each other, as well as with me, and produced eventually 180 typed pages of evidence, most of it four-letter words. I was lucky to get bail. As I waited to appear before the magistrates, the police constable accompanying me said, 'I

40

believe you are a very concerned person, who got too involved in a difficult situation, and ended up breaking the
law.' Not even my parents were as understanding as that.

Two Quaker families offered me a temporary home, as the
magistrates were unwilling for me to live alone. In the
event I was able to take advantage of both offers, so that
the bail period was an enriching time, and by no means totally sad. I wrote letters to almost everyone I knew, telling
them what had happened and what the prospects were. I agreed
with the suggestion of a psychiatrist to take the drug
Androcur, which is supposed to reduce sexual drive, but in
my case caused breast enlargement and a lot of discomfort.

During the bail period I was committed for trial on charges of gross indecency with the three younger boys, then
aged twenty, seventeen and twelve. The Director of Public
Prosecutions did not propose any charge with regard to the
eldest, who at twenty-two was now beyond the scope of that
particular law.

A colourful selection of my friends turned up for the
trial at the Crown Court; I wished very much that they had
come for my wedding instead. I heard afterwards that the
usher asked them what I had done, and then told them that
with that particular judge, imprisonment was certain.

As it happened, the trial was totally irregular. I knew
what charges to expect, and had indicated that I should be
pleading guilty. But the dates of some of the charges were
altered, to make the boys look younger than they were, and
an additional, more serious charge was brought with regard
to the eldest, which was introduced illegally: for a start,
the DPP had not authorised it, and there were technical
grounds why it could not be brought (eg date of offence
longer ago in the past than the time limit of twelve months).
I was appalled to see the way my honest admission was exploited by men with fewer moral scruples than I had myself;
when enforcing a law, it is particularly important to use
legal methods to do so, and not to alienate impartial opinion by making criminals into martyrs.

The prosecution counsel not only drew attention to the
illegality of my behaviour, but ridiculed it. The judge was
openly hostile to my headmaster and the eminent psychiatrist
who were the first witnesses for the defence, making it
clear that they were wasting the time of the Court and the
real decisions had been taken behind the scenes. As his
voice took on the ecclesiastical chanting note, 'The sentence I am about to pass upon you...', it suddenly came to
me that the man sitting up there in his robes saw himself
as some kind of High Priest. Yet he seemed so vulnerable;
there was something about the case that frightened him.
'You will go to prison for four years.'

I am told that a gasp ran round the Court; I only know
that I was jolted down the steps by two henchmen who would
have done the same for any other convicted prisoner. My
father, who had no sympathy at all for the difficulties I
had caused myself, was openly angry at the course of the
trial. I was visited at once by a lady probation officer,
who asked me if there were any last requests (she did not

say that). I asked her to telephone my mother, who was not in Court but waiting at the home of friends. My solicitor also came to see me in the cage, and said there were grounds for appeal.

My adventures in prison make a chapter in themselves. The first few days were much the worst part. I was in our local prison, where the reason for my presence was known and I had to be kept in solitary confinement, both for my own protection and to preserve good order among the other men. I discovered at once that prison officers are as anxious as teachers about that sort of thing. I found the officers' foul language hard to take; I thought, 'This isn't my world; this is a big mistake; I must look on it as an educational experience, and make the most of it.'

During those first terrible few days, I was aware of being cut off not only from the normal community outside but from what I could see was a supportive environment inside the prison. The doctor did not try to hide his distaste at having to examine me. Some men threatened me with lurid abuse through the locked door of my cell, but one returned several times to say, 'Are you appealing? Your sentence is far too long.' In fact the Appeals Officer visited me before I had even got round to sending for him, and a well-spoken officer said to me in a quiet moment, 'Don't take any notice of what some of the men say to you; it's their way of coming to terms with the bad things they've done themselves.' And I shall always remember that the local Quaker prison visitor, who happened to be a personal friend anyway, came to see me almost as soon as I arrived.

After four days I was moved to another prison where I was not known; the Deputy Governor met me on arrival, and advised me not to talk about my case at all, but if pressed to tell other men I was an accountant in for fraud. In practice, 'What you in for?' is a standard opening to prison conversation, and I almost got to believe in the end that I was actually in for fraud. I stood higher in the pecking order than you might think, because I was serving so long; obviously a very large sum of money must have been involved; for a first offender to get four years was unheard of.

This deception, which earlier on I should not have been able to manage, enabled me to live as a normal prisoner, and at the time this seemed like a deliverance. I felt a special bond towards the two men with whom I shared that first night, one a young chap in for the theft of a TV set, the other for attacking his estranged wife. Most of the men were younger than I was, in fact for a short time I had a boy as a cellmate; I realised that not only did the other inmates not know the reason why I was there, most of the officers did not know either. I survived several rumours which came perilously near the truth. I was dismayed to see the first two men with whom I shared a permanent cell were people I should have nothing in common with; in fact one of them later attacked me and blacked my eye; I have never known why. This happened at night, I rang the emergency bell and was moved at once. Next day I was offered a move to another prison, but declined this, saying, 'I'm only just

getting to know people here.' I also asked that no procee-
dings should be taken against the man who had gone for me,
as it would only have stirred up more trouble. This epi-
sode, I now see, marked the moment when I began to recover
some self-respect; my attitude was very well received. After
that I had a superior cell with only two beds. I also coped
better with the moods of desperate unhappiness which had
disturbed other men. These moods began with certain observable signs and I realised after a time that when I began
to go down, so to speak, one of the other men came unobtru-
sively and talked with me until I picked up again.
    I survived as well as I did for a variety of good reasons.
The Welfare Officer was a sympathetic young woman and an
ally from the start. I had a visit every twenty-eight days,
from friends who were Quakers or whose children I had taught
over the years. The local Quaker visitor came each week,
once absent-mindedly asking for his own cell where he had
spent time thirty years before as a conscientious objector.
We held a short meeting for worship, with another Quaker
prisoner, an older and more embittered man than I was. To
me, the inanities of institutional life seemed all too fam-
iliar. Prison life was extremely monotonous, especially at
weekends when we were 'banged up' almost the whole time,
but it involved a lot less day-to-day stress than teaching
in a comprehensive school, where the demands on me had been
so multifarious that I increasingly failed to make any real
progress at all. I slept a lot, especially at first. I was
well fed in prison, which is ironical in a world where half
the people are starving. The diet included much more meat
and fish than I could afford ouside.
    We were given work to do, but I was found to be so stu-
pid that I had to be given the least skilled job in the
tailors' shop, which could be done with scissors. The repe-
titious work was therapeutic at first. Later I was given a
workmate in for the same thing as I was, an act of compas-
sion on someone's part. We were able to talk at times. Then
I was promoted to Chapel Orderly, thanks to the Chaplain
who also became my friend, and whose services I attended
each Sunday. This job brought privileges; though I had less
to spend at the prison canteen, I could make tea or coffee
at any time, and play the organ, and unlike my predecessor
I did not drink the communion wine. My work involved clean-
ing and dusting, but also welcoming visitors and providing
quiet ecumenical liaison between all connected with the
Chapel. There were conferences and a week's mission, supported by members of local churches. I am sure that the
Prison Chapel was a force for good in some men's lives, and
that this sprang from the personal popularity of the Chaplain.
    People say, 'Didn't you feel the shame of being sent to
prison?' Well, yes, of course one does, though my first
reaction was shock and after that it was a question of survival. The shame part of the sentence was served mostly by
my parents. On the other hand, I got impatient with well-
wishers who saw me as some sort of martyr. It was my own
stupidity and lack of sense of proportion that had got me

43

behind bars, and the experience gave me more worldly wisdom, as well as a deeper insight into other human beings.

There were unexpected benefits of prison life, all of them far from the mind of the judge who sent me there. I had no idea how much simpler it is to live without handling money. There were many moments of good fellowship, and for the first time I coped effectively with an all-male institution. I was valued after a time because I could translate Latin mottoes and spell long words, just as others were valued because they were clever at model-making or painting. Towards the end, a disgruntled prison officer told some men why I was in prison, and I was threatened, but my immediate neighbours on my landing closed ranks to protect me, and nothing happened. By then they were no longer interested in why I was there; I was accepted as a whole person.

Prisoners talk of 'paying their debt to society' - I have no time for this, at a cost of £100 a week. My trial and imprisonment cost about £4000, of which I paid nothing. The punishment did nothing to help the people I had wronged, if by that you mean the boys in the case. If you mean the judge, then I suppose it did do something. I learned from other men a certain stoicism; many of them, in real terms, were in much worse circumstances, and had been in and out of trouble all their lives. One reason why sending me to prison had such an element of overkill was that I had no previous convictions at all - not even a parking fine.

Prisons are supposed to be hotbeds of homosexuality, but I saw no evidence of this at all. If I was 'depraved and corrupted', it was by the hard porn displayed on the noticeboards in some men's cells; I could see that this was only an assertion of virility and part of the prison sub-culture, but it alienated me from the female body in a way I had never been before.

My appeal was twice postponed, and finally heard forty weeks after my trial. The hearing at the Law Courts lasted five minutes. A few days earlier I was instructed to attend in person, which the Principal Officer told me was a very good sign. I was taken to London by hired car, by a driver and two officers: a far cry from the days when Quaker prisoners went from one gaol to another on foot, carrying their mittimuses in their hands. The Lord Chief Justice upheld my appeal, quashing my conviction on the most serious charge. As I had already served over my time on the others, that meant that I had to be released at once. A door was unlocked, and there I was. My first feeling was of fear of all the crowds moving along the pavement in the Strand, though they knew nothing of me.

After a few days I returned to my former home, which caused no difficulties as there was some feeling locally that I had been badly treated; a sympathetic account of the trial in the local paper had helped me here. I was able to get casual work almost at once, and benefited socially very much from my new job, though I had to give it up after six months when I found I was trying to live off less than I should have got on Social Security, and my savings were trickling away. For a time I had a Saturday job as well, to

try to balance the books, but this almost broke me. If
Social Security had been prepared to pay my fares to work,
that would have made all the difference. I got very demor-
alised when I realised that they had no interest in whether
I worked or not. I have been unable to find a permanent job
since my release from prison, though here again, I am in a
stronger position than many men would be, as I can fill my
time without trying, on Friends' work and my own numerous
interests. I have had wonderful support from people in local
Meetings, and have been able to discuss my difficulties
(though that was coming about even before all this happened;
the situation is more urgent now·, as if I get four years
for a first offence, what will it be next time?). My relationship with my parents is certainly closer than it was.
I miss the company of young people; it is like losing a
limb, and I am so desperate about this at times, I try not
to think about it. Yet the end of this preoccupation has
freed energies for other sides of my life which interest
me as much.

I have seen all the 'boys' since my release; they are
used to crises and suffered less than I did. The eldest is
now twenty-five and I attended his wedding. I have met the
mother also, and feel no resentment towards her at all;
only astonishment that it was really necessary for all this
to happen.

I have had some contact with former school colleagues,
and more support was offered; but we don't have much in common any more. Some former pupils have gone out of their way
to help me. I would also have been accepted among local
groups with openly-professed homosexual preferences, but I
do not feel I have much in common with them either, though
I enjoy discussion on such topics as the age of consent
which is of such obvious concern at present. I have none
of the characteristics popularly associated with the term
'homosexual', though I would say that the way life has worked
out has given me, instead of the traditional male aggression, an increasing sense of care for the individual, and
in particular an intense sympathy for the plight of growing
youngsters, more especially boys. The whole business of
emotion and sex has come to relate, for me, far more to
the growth and emergence of personality than to relationships between mature people. I am sorry if that makes me
a threat to society; sorry too that the Secretary for Education and Science dismissed me with a bald note, containing
threats, and included no word of thanks for what I had done
for my pupils in the past, or of good wishes for the future.

I will conclude with some general observations. First I
must say that I deplore the way that the moral overtones of
the sexual side of life still inhibit any rational discussion of things that must be of importance to all of us, and
inhibits young people's growth to maturity. By 'maturity' I
do not just mean successful marriage and parenthood - which
I insist is the option almost all of us would choose, given
any choice in the matter - but to a maturity of attitude
which while avoiding antisocial behaviour on its own account,
would also avoid undue morbid preoccupation with the short-

comings of others. The present hysteria that 'sex cases' attract is a pointer to widespread guilt; very many people know that there is a streak of waywardness in themselves, in sexual as in other matters, and they cannot bring themselves to acknowledge it. That is why the involvement of the law can have such terrible results; it brings into the most delicate area of human relationships the heavy-handed intervention of outsiders whose only reaction can be to act out their own repressions.

Finally, I must mention that I was present in court recently when the same judge who sentenced me gave a former pupil of mine a twelve-month suspended sentence for battering his baby son. There were extenuating circumstances - illness, low intelligence, and the young man will have to support the baby for many years, though he will never see it again. But having said all that, the thought stays with me that a fractured skull was involved - the baby could have died - and the sentence seems lenient after what that same man awarded me. I think it points to the fact that our society, in spite of what is said about opposing violence, is in fact more tolerant of violent acts than of irregular loving. There is a reason for this. Our society is concerned with power - I deplore this, but it is true. Love corrupts in a way that violence does not; violence can be stopped with greater violence, but love is insidious and makes people vulnerable.

The real corruption is shown by the cheapening of human beings, by such things as the meat displayed on Page Three of a popular paper. Such things depress the tone of our culture and encourage the idea that people are there to be used and controlled. Popular acceptance of such attitudes provides the atmosphere in which extreme exploiters such as rapists and rippers can operate. They are only acting out in spectacular and self-seeking terms what society encourages us all to think women are for. Compared to this sort of thing, a caring relationship, however idiosyncratic, can easily be recognised because it enhances the personalities involved.

I believe the age of consent for homosexual acts between males should be eighteen, as recommended by the Policy Advisory Committee on Sexual Offences. Below that age there should only be prosecution when someone has been clearly hurt or exploited. No good can come of laying open to view things that could be dealt with far more reasonably by guidance and support.

To devote the amount of time and trouble to the oppression of sexual irregularities, in young people as well as adults, that happened in my case amounts in itself to a 'corruption of public morals'. Most people do not think these things of such prime importance; they have more immediate problems to worry about, and it is not to the credit of the law that it persists in attracting so much attention to things that only touch a few people's lives.

11 Christine Edwards & Valerie Grist

I first heard the word 'homosexual' when I was fourteen. I
was composing an ode on the virtues of my History mistress,
during a particularly boring Biology lesson, when the girl
in the next desk whispered,'There's a name for people like
you,' and proceeded to tell me what it was. It took three
years for me to accept that it applied to me, and a further
seven to come to terms with it. During all this time I remained in love with the History mistress, suffering agonies
when I saw less of her on leaving school, and finally lost
contact when she emigrated. I was very lonely during those
ten years. Lonely because I felt I must be the only homosexual in the world, and would never be able to tell anyone
about myself. Lonely because my friends got engaged and
married and couldn't understand why I never had boyfriends.
And lonely because I thought I was doomed to be on my own
for ever. I took my first job as far from home as possible,
threw myself into committees and evening classes, and set
out to prove to myself and the world how self-sufficient
I was.

My first inkling that other people had had similar experiences came with reading Radclyffe Hall's The Well of Loneliness. The relief which flooded over me on reading of
emotions with which I could identify far outweighed the
embarrassment it had cost me to order the book from the
library! Similar relief came with the magazine Arena Three,
obtained after reading an article by Bryan Magee in
The Guardian. Here at last were love stories which weren't
all 'the wrong way round', here was correspondence about
the sort of feelings I actually experienced.

Social gatherings were arranged through Arena Three,
and I eventually got myself to one, organised by a delight-
ful Australian girl in Putney. It's hard to believe now
that I had never before met any gay women, and was actually
scared of doing so. I had the media's stereotyped image of
cropped hair and a tie, and was genuinely frightened that
I would be the only one in a skirt and nail varnish! I spent
half an hour walking round the block before getting up the
courage to knock on the door. I'm eternally grateful that
Ididn't give up and take the next train home, because at
that first meeting I met Val. It was a year before we could
change jobs and set up home together, and in that year I
seemed to crowd in all that I had missed as a teenager. We
met in cafes and clubs, we danced and bought singles of
'our' tunes, we spent a fortune on phone calls and letters,
and then we exchanged rings and settled down.

I stretched luxuriously and sat up in bed. It was the first
day of the school holidays, and I had just completed my
probationary year as a teacher. So now I could relax, with
six weeks of idling about, knowing that I was now qualified
and so had no more worries about teaching. (Well, not so
many worries over teaching!) I had collected a pile of

47

magazines to read, and looked forward to breakfast in bed,
a browse through the latest gossip, and getting up late,
while other poor souls were working.

I happened to look through the personal column of the
New Statesman, and read 'Arena Three, a magazine for homosexual women' (or some such advert). Immediately I felt as
if I had been kicked smartly on the head! Maybe that's
what I was. I never seemed to fit in anywhere, so maybe I
was one of those odd women I had occasionally read about,
although since I had never had the faintest desire to crop
my hair or wear a tie, maybe I wasn't. But no harm in trying. I answered the advertisement, received Arena Three,
answered an advert in that for 'shy members' and within
two months had met Chris and realised that wearing a tie
was not a necessary part of the homosexual way of life!

I was thirty-three when I realised I was gay. During my
school days in the 1940s and 1950s, it was considered quite
normal to adore the sixth form, and no one had a boyfriend
in my class even at seventeen years of age. I had no idea
what sin Oscar Wilde had committed, and it never occurred
to me that there was any alternative to love and marriage
with the opposite sex. In fact, love without marriage was
daring enough, and the idea of loving the same sex never
crossed my mind.

In my twenties, I did my best to conform, trying to get
up enthusiasm for boyfriends and marriage. All my friends
married, I got engaged once, but just couldn't bring myself
to carry it through, even to please my parents, who by
this time were getting outspokenly critical. I felt that
by agreeing to marry ―― (I regret to say I've forgotten
his name) I would become less than myself, and would have
to deny part of myself. I could never define what I meant,
even to myself, and never realised until later that the
chief emotion I felt when out with any man was fear - utter
and complete terror whenever they made any physical overtures. So in my late twenties, I gave up all ideas of sex
and marriage - not for me, I said loudly and crossly to my
parents. I travelled to New Zealand, I busily did things,
and then I decided to get a job I would be able to keep all
my life, and which would always be interesting and demanding. So I trained to teach.

During all this time, homosexuality was slowly becoming
more openly discussed. The terminology changed, people
ceased being 'queer' and became 'gay'. The idea that women
as well as men could be gay slowly percolated into my sub-
conscious. And so the moment of understanding arrived, at
the time I had the energy and the strength to cope with all
that it entailed. Once I met others who were gay, I immediately felt that in their company I fitted in, I was not
the odd one looking in from outside. At last there were
parties I enjoyed, and the pleasure just to be with others
like myself was quite overwhelming.

We have now been together for over thirteen years, and
really do give thanks for the happiness these years have
brought us. By many standards we must seem conventional and

even boring: we do believe in fidelity; we do prefer doing
things together rather than apart; we have grown so alike
that we frequently anticipate each other's thoughts; and
we regard our relationship as a marriage 'till death us do
part'. We know this type of partnership wouldn't be right
for everyone, but it happens to work for us.

We've derived enormous joy from all the hobbies and interests we have shared with each other. We both feel we've
changed under the influence of the other - one of us to the
extent of training for and embarking on a new career. We've
developed together a great concern over ecology, conserva-
tion and natural resources, which led us to join the Ecology Party. Similarly, our coming to the Society of Friends
was the result of searching, reading and discussing together,
and we feel it to be important that we do agree on fundamental issues like this.

We like to be accepted socially as a 'couple'. While
not rushing in to announce our homosexuality to new acquaintances, we don't lie about it, and hope that our friends
will slowly come to a tacit understanding. This certainly
seems to be the case: friends who already know and care
for us are not affected by the news that we are gay. We
entertain and are entertained as a 'married' couple; our
meeting made us joint treasurers, and when the subject
happened to arise, they expressed no surprise, and appeared
to have already guessed.

Although we see our relationship as a marriage, we don't
have clearly defined roles. Neither of us regularly wears
the trousers, either literally or metaphorically; we share
most tasks, and where we divide them the division certainly
isn't sexist ; the one who drives the car can't hammer in
a nail!

For the past two years only one of us has worked (in a
school for the mentally handicapped) while the other spends
half the week on voluntary work, and also runs the house
and garden, and does the decorating. This leads to great
difficulty over answering the standard question 'What do
you do?' for the one at home. 'I used to teach' seems hardly
adequate, 'I'm just a housewife' is definitely out, 'I do
voluntary work' sounds too good to be true, and so 'Nothing'
is the easiest answer!

But for us this arrangement has been a complete liberation. There is no sense of being 'trapped' in the house, in
that it is a purely voluntary decision and could be rever-
sed. School work, lesson preparation and so on are disposed
of while supper is prepared and cleared, leaving both of us
with more time. We have acquired a family of three cats
and a dog (and an open door to strays!) now that one of us
is at home all day. And best of all we have acquired time
- to walk, to read, to be more active in meeting, and to
discover in middle age a passion for horse-riding!

We have a number of gay friends, and we greatly value
the fellowship of FHF and our local Gay Christian Movement
group. It is still reassuring to be with people who understand your way of life, and with whom you can be completely
honest. It is also important to keep such groups running,

for those newly coming to terms with their sexuality and
so needing somewhere to turn. However, we spend relatively
little of our spare time with gays, and our friends are
chiefly made through our other activities and interests.
We are not great campaigners, and have virtually forgotten
that we belong to a minority. Most of the time, being gay
seems as unimportant as being left-handed. Let us hope that
at some time in the future every gay will be accepted by
the whole of society, and all discussion of gayness really
will be irrelevant.

12 Tom Bodine

I grew up in a Quaker community in Philadelphia, Pennsyl-
vania in the 1920s and 1930s. I attended a Quaker meeting
and Quaker Sunday School and received my primary and secondary education at a Quaker day school and my university
education at a small Methodist university. Mine was a
totally sheltered existence. I never heard the word 'homosexual' until I was twenty-eight years old and happened on
a book called The Psychology of Sex.
    I knew I was different but had no idea why. I couldn't
understand why I got no charge out of holding a girl in my
arms while dancing. Kissing a girl was a fearsome thought,
and when I tried it on taking home a 'date' at the end of
an evening or on the occasion of a university dance weekend, it was both disagreeable and embarrassing. Yet when
I touched a boy or happened one time to play the role of a
girl in a fraternity play and found myself embracing a boy,
I felt a thrill that is indescribable in words. In fact, I
had a problem in the showers of my college fraternity; the
effect on me of showering with other boys was so embarrassing I had to choose odd times of the day or night to shower
when there was no one else around. If I stood next to a boy
or young man on a crowded bus I felt waves of electricity;
pressing against a girl or young woman meant nothing.
    I remember asking my best friend at university why I
felt nothing when I was on a date with a girl; how did one
learn to kiss somebody as I saw everyone around me doing?
He told me not to worry; it would come when I met the right
girl, the girl intended for me. When I was twenty-eight
years old and had discovered from the book mentioned above
that there were a few unfortunate people in the world who
were attracted physically only to their own sex, I remember
consulting our family physician about it, a man I liked
and trusted. I remember how taken aback he was by the question, how he walked over to the window of his office and
stood looking out of it with his back to me, and his turning to me and saying, 'Don't worry; this is a phase many
young men go through; you will grow out of it.'
    Some years later, in 1949, I had a run-in with ulcers
and spent a month convalescing in glorious hot summer
weather with a family on Martha's Vineyard Island off the
coast of Massachusetts. I spent the time - on the beach,

playing tennis, sailing a boat - with the daughter of the
family, a girl in her twenties, a beautiful girl whom I
loved being with. One evening, in the moonlight (!), she
made overtures and I rebuffed her, and when we joined the
family around the kitchen talbe for our evening cocoa, her
mother sized up the situation and wrote on a pad the words
Ecce Homo and pushed it across to her husband. The following day I was walking far up the beach, miles away from
other people, and came across a boy sunbathing in the nude
behind a dune. He was not in the least abashed by my arrival
and signalled me to join him. My heart was pounding and I
lay down on the warm sand next to him, and, as the saying
goes, 'one little thing led to another'.

The next few hours were among the happiest I have ever
spent. He told me about the gay world, and how natural it
is for some men to love other men and how a relationship
between two men can be as fulfilling, as enduring and as
wholesome as one between a man and a woman. I never saw
the boy again, but beginning with that day on the beach
at Martha's Vineyard, I have slowly but steadily learned
to feel good about myself and about my sexual orientation.
I have been blessed over the years with two long-term relationships and with many, many short-term ones. There have
been down-times, of course, as there are, I feel sure, in
all human relationships, but, over all, I have been happy
as a homosexual, despite the myriad problems of living
out a lie in an often cruel and heartless heterosexual
society.

I am told I should not use such strong terms as 'cruel
and heartless'. Perhaps not. The words seem valid to me.
Which of my life experiences can I describe that might help
non-homosexuals to understand what it is like (or has been
like) to be homosexual in a heterosexual society? I worked
for thirty-nine years for a large insurance company in
Hartford, Connecticut. I was successful in my job as liaison
with the State Insurance Departments. I seemed to have a
special gift for getting favourable decisions for my company from the government bureaucracies who controlled us.
After fifteen or twenty years, I was in line for promotion
to be a director ('officer' in American terminology) of
the company at a really good salary with beautiful 'perks'.
But the promotion never came. My contemporaries in other
companies doing similar work were Vice-Presidents and even
Presidents of the smaller companies. At one time I was
chairman of no fewer than eleven nation-wide industry committees concerned with getting favourable decisions from
State governments, committees composed entirely of directors
of other companies.

I finally consulted a friend who was a major shareholder
as well as a top director of the company, and he agreed
at once with my feeling that I had been wrongfully passed
over for promotion. He looked up my personnel file and
talked with one or two of my superiors and came back to me
with the appalling (as it seemed to me then) news that my
movements in the homosexual underground of the time, which
I thought had been totally quiet and discreet, were known

51

to the company through the periodic 'inspection' reports they secured on executive-level employees from time to time. It had been decided not to confront me with this information but just to let it lie.

My top-level friend advised me not to make an issue of it. The company had been very good to me over the years. had given me 'military' leave of absence during World War II as a conscientious objector, and my job itself was secure (as long as I remained discreet). I was too valuable an employee to dismiss. In those days there were no gay liberation movements, no anti-discrimination laws and no gay support groups, Quaker or otherwise. So I decided to accept it as one of those things. I liked my work. I liked the people I worked with. And I was in the midst of a particularly happy long-term personal relationship. Being a director of the company with a big salary and nice 'perks' didn't seem all that important. (I did become a junior-level director five years before my retirement, when the climate in the community had become a bit less homophobic and when it was evident that my personal lifestyle, quiet and discreet as it was, was unlikely to embarrass the company.)

But there were constantly things I found hard to take living in a 'Christian' society that required me to deny myself and to live out a lie, by pretending that I was heterosexual when I wasn't. When the men I associated with in business told jokes about 'pansies' and 'faggots', I cringed but said nothing. When I attended the encounter groups and consciousness-raising sessions which were all the rage in America in the 1960s, I found it embarrassing to embrace or massage women as was expected of male members of such groups, or, even more embarrassing, to be massaged or embraced by eager-beaver females. I could, of course, have just avoided such groups, but they were hard to avoid on Quaker retreat weekends which in other respects I enjoyed.

For three years from 1972 to 1975, following a five-year term as Clerk of my own Yearly Meeting in New England, I served as Presiding Clerk of Friends United Meeting, that great body of middle-of-the-road, mainly pastoral, mainly 'Christ-centred' Friends headquartered in Richmond, Indiana, with 100,000 members extending around the world from East Africa to California. Some of the Friends on the FUM Executive Committee and FUM General Board over which I presided came from a fundamentalist Quaker background. From time to time they expressed their feelings about the 'sin of homosexuality' in strong language. For example one of them wrote an editorial for his Yearly Meeting's monthly bulletin entitled 'The Kingdom of God and the Homosexual' which read in part as follows:

'A very clear line was drawn by Paul, by direction of the Holy Spirit. Excluded from the kingdom of God were those who were practising homosexuality...Any person, be he a homosexual, an adulterer, a thief, a drunkard, a slanderer, a swindler, or any other practising sinner is not in Christ or the kingdom of God. If this is strong language it is because

it is biblical language...Let there be no uncertainty
as to the position of our Yearly Meeting with
reference to homosexuality. Homosexuality is a sin.'
A later editorial entitled 'The Homosexual and Human
Rights' went on to say:
'There is just as much hope for the homosexual offender
as there is for the prostitute and the supreme
task of the church in this respect is to hold
out the hope of redemption and new life in Christ.
Many homosexuals have now come out from behind
closet doors. They are admitting their homosexual
practices and demanding their rights. What rights
do they have? What rights do prostitutes have? What
rights do thieves have? What rights do murderers
have? What rights do drunkards have? What rights
do slanderers have? If any one objects to these sinful practices being all lumped together - as though
one were as bad as another - let them discuss it
with God. It's God's word which classifies all these
practices as being sinful (1 Corinthians 6:9-10).'
What should I have done as Clerk of FUM? Should I have declared my homosexuality and have hoped for understanding? I
decided it was best 'to live out a lie', not from cowardice,
I like to think, but because my being 'out' to gay Friends
and 'closeted' to straight Friends enabled me to be a go-
between and help both sides grow in understanding. At the
Friends General Conference at Ithaca in 1972 and again at
the Conference of All Friends in the Americas in 1977,
there were confrontations over homosexuality that could
have caused further 'separations' in the Society of Friends
in America. I was a member of the Steering Committee of
those gatherings. The fact that I was respected by Friends
on both sides permitted me to play a role that helped
towards changing the atmosphere from one of confrontation
to one of growth in understanding.
    This is the first time I have written about my life as
a homosexual in a heterosexual society. Perhaps what I have
written will explain why I am such a devotee of Friends
Homosexual Fellowship in Great Britain and of the Friends
Committee on Gay and Lesbian Concerns in America, why I
worked so hard over so many years on the Human Sexuality
Working Pary of the Friends General Conference in Philadelphia, why I helped to raise money in 1975 for the reprinting
of Towards a Quaker View of Sex at a time when it was out
of print, why I helped to organise a committee of the local
Council of Churches in Hartford, Connecticut, whose purpose
was to arrange wholesome places for gays to meet, why I
have shared in several meetings for worship held to bless
the union of gay couples, why I long for appropriate changes
in our Quaker Book of Discipline, and why I rejoiced in the
decision of London Yearly Meeting 1981 to take up the issue
of sexuality and sexual orientation in small groups at the
local meeting level.
    I long for the day when no young Friend anywhere need
go through what I went through up to the age of thirty-four,
when all Friends oriented as I am may have the chance to

receive the blessings that have been mine, without the need, in Quaker circles at least, of living out a lie.

13 John Shackleton

The feeling of being alone - that, I think, is the main impression of being homosexual in my youth, indeed until I was forty-two. I was an only child and a birthright Friend. Because of the age structure of my parents' families (they were both the youngest of large families stretching over twenty years), I was accustomed to all relatives being 'old' - even now I cannot accustom myself to the idea that one can be a grandparent in one's forties. So I mixed most of the time with older people.

I had very few friends at school and those I had were like me, the few who did not shine at sports or other 'manly' activities. It was, however, not with them that I indulged in adolescent sex talk and mutual masturbation. For those activities I had sporadic entree into a wider group of boys. Mine was a boys' school. I never remember receiving any sex education from my parents or at school. I discovered in a cupboard some Victorian or Edwardian pamphlets which condemned the sin of self-abuse and all its horrific consequences. Somewhere I learned the word 'homosexual' (and thought 'homo' was Latin for 'man' not Greek for 'same'). 'Gay' was not vernacular in my youth. I suppose I applied the word to myself from the mid teens, but I had no understanding of what it really meant. I knew I had no desire whatever to get married and that I had no interest in girls. But I can't say that my contemporaries were interested in girls either. Dating and courtship were activities for twenties, not teens. Only when I was at university was I aware of 'going out with girls', but the fact that I didn't aroused no comment. I suppose that in these few sentences I have indicated the extent of the revolution in such mores since the 1940s and early 1950s.

I always fantasised about men. I recall admiring other boys' looks at primary school and can remember the names of at least three of these boys. One has the same name as a famous actor, but I have never discovered if he and the boy are one and the same. I was brought up virtually as teetotal - certainly pubs and social drinking were out. I suppose there were 'gay' pubs in those days, but I didn't know and had no way of finding out. There was no place to my knowledge where homosexuals could meet, let alone indulge in sexual activity. Quite accidentally, I discovered public lavatories as meeting places for sex. I had some sort of intuition that they might be. By dint of constant visitations, I found those where such activity was commonplace. Homosexual trysting in public conveniences - 'cottaging' as it is termed by the cognoscenti - is for some men, but not for women, a worldwide practice, and has even been the subject of scholarly sociological research.

I look back on the twenty years or more during which I

indulged in this activity with distaste now, but obviously I cannot and do not condemn it. I admit its squalor and sadness. It is still illegal, as homosexual activity is only legal, amongst many other conditions, in private. Somehow, it is my feeling that it is a much more dangerous activity than it used to be. Not only do the police seem to be more generally watchful, but they employ <u>agents provocateurs</u> more widely and resort to numerous antics and gambits to trap the unwary and, often, the entirely innocent. There is also a greater chance of being mugged by 'queer-bashers'.

It must be frankly admitted that cottaging is addictive like a drug. Once one is aware that sex, however furtive, is likely to be found from resort to a particular convenience, one is drawn back time and again. Probably to the surprise of many readers, quite a proportion of 'cottagers' are not truly homosexual, for many married men are attracted to sexual release in this way. Mutual masturbation is much more fun that a solo effort, quite apart from other sexual needs which marriage does not necessarily fulfil for many men. Cottaging is attractive in that, given the 'come-on' sign by nod, wink or other movement, sexual contact can be immediate. It may not be private and may not allow of more than straightforward masturbation or oral sex. There is a frequent camaraderie amongst cottagers in that if a pair do decide to operate together, others will watch out for potential intruders whilst themselves gaining pleasure from voyeurism. There are, strangely, many who are excited by the element of danger involved. The London Underground stations on my way from home to university each day proved fertile hunting grounds, and wherever I went subsequently to live or visit, I developed an instinct as to which were probably the places to go.

But much furtive sex is anonymous. The majority of cottagers have nowhere else to go, but few such contacts wanted to talk and even fewer led to going to their homes and the comfort of bed. Only in the latter years did I have a place to take such people myself. Very few people did I meet more than once or twice.

But it was talking of which I was deprived; hence the loneliness and isolation I referred to at the start. I culd seldom talk to my homosexual contacts. I certainly couldn't talk to family or friends. I just suffered in silent torment. The law condemned all my activities as criminal and society concurred with the law. I felt guilty. I felt sure I would be disowned by the Society of Friends if ever I was discovered in my wickedness.

Apart from occasional early reference to 'Miss Right's turning up one day', my parents mercifully never pressed the point about marriage and must, I assume, have eventually accepted the fact that I was a confirmed bachelor, even a 'gay' bachelor in the proper use of that term. I eschewed all social contacts that meant dancing or 'going with girls'. I had a few friends to whom I owe a great debt of gratitude. I lived a life that was full of activity for work, the Society of Friends and such socialising as coffee with friends or theatre trips. I went out almost every Saturday

for trips on my own, and spent most of my holidays by myself,
usually on package tours where there luckily turned out to
be someone else on his own to talk to. I never knew whether
those holiday companions were gay - it is likely some were.
Sometimes these companions were older women, with whom I
have always got on very well as they posed no sexual threat,
or married couples.

Liberation from all this came with the publication in
The Friend of an anonymous article 'Homosexuality from the
Inside' in the summer of 1971. I was almost forty-two. I
wrote to the editor and eventually David Blamires, the
author, got in touch with me. I also joined the Campaign
for Homosexual Equality and shall never forget the first
time I walked into a room at a befriending meeting in
Ealing knowing everyone else there was gay and a soul kin-
dred to myself. I also recall correspondence in The Friend
following the article, much of it critical, and one letter
in particular which wondered what would happen if a meeting
discovered that its clerk was gay. I was Clerk at Kensington
Meeting at the time, and in my guilt, I wondered indeed!

Now my life has changed dramatically. Of course I still
hide myself from some people but I have been open with many
others and have almost cried with relief at the loving acceptance extended to me. Things have not always been easy and
I haven't found a partner, but I praise God for my wonderful
friends, true friends I'm sure with mutual love and caring
between us.

My story is no different from countless others. Sadly
there are many others still suffering as I did, not only of
my generation but also amongst the young. Even in these
freer days there is still a stigma attached to gayness and
the condition is woefully misunderstood. I have been lucky
and found Friends to be friends, but I know with others
this may sadly not always prove to be the case. Remember,
please, Friends, in all charity the loneliness of a homosexual in a heterosexually oriented culture and extend to
him or her the hand of friendship and acceptance.

14 Alastair Milne

I have been shaken out of my comfortable beliefs by the
experiences of the last few years. During this time I
accepted that I was gay and in finding my own identity
and sexuality my humanisation was complete.

I do not, at the time of writing, have a committed gay
relationship but I hope that this will happen in the full-
ness of time. This is not the story of my coming out but
rather thoughts on the position which my relationship with
the Society of Friends has reached.

The instinctive approach of Friends is through the feelings and experience of present-day human beings and the
God in them rather than through texts or reliance on theology. Whilst Friends' thinking on sexuality is far in advance
of other Christian denominations, we are not in unity on the

question of acceptance of gay people. I have 'come out' in my own meeting at Watford, and in the loving and caring situation which exists at that meeting I found it a liberating experience.

Gayness in people should be so accepted as to be totally unimportant. I feel that this hope is, however, Utopian. Imagine, if you will, people who grow up in a world òr society to which they feel they do not belong because of their homosexuality - and because of this, the difficulty of gaining self-respect.

In gay groups, a strong fellowship has been developed from which a gay person can find a new strength; and the ensuing security means that she or he will find a welcoming openness which will allow that person to develop and bind together the strands of humanity and sexuality and become a whole person. However, the situation there has to be compared with the plight of the gay person in the real world. It has been estimated that the wholly or partially gay population of Great Britain is ten to thirteen per cent - about two million five hundred thousand - and of these only around seven thousand belong to any kind of gay group.

Friends do not as a whole discriminate against gays. This led me to believe that I would not be shunned by fellow Quakers and this has been the case. There are meetings which I understand do not respond with the same love, care and understanding with which I have been met. There are gays in the Society who have not felt sufficiently strengthened by the Christian faith and practice in the experience of a particular meeting to declare themselves. The vital opportunity for friendship in the true context of their respective sexuality has then been missed.

I do feel that gays are beginning to feel more accepted by the Society, but this is a slow process of chipping away bit by bit as knowledge grows. As Friends' personal knowledge of gays increases this can give rise to solid thinking in this area by individual Friends and the Society as a whole which will by personal experience dispel any remaining prejudice, distrust, fear and ignorance that still remains.

Alongside the work that gay groups are doing and will need to continue to do, the Society can contribute towards the building up of relationships and right thinking. We may not thus reconstruct a theology but we may be doing something far more vital both for ourselves and for others: not only by doing this but by declaring where we stand as a Society in accepting gay people as they are - not only from inside the Society, but from outside as well.

15 Irene Jacoby

I was born in Danzig, and my early years were spent there in an orthodox Jewish family. I was somewhat aware of what this meant, of course, but it did not impinge upon my childhood. I think of my childhood as being as ordinary

as one would expect in a fairly rich Jewish family, where I
was brought up as much by my nannies as by my mother. I do
remember my parents, however, though I have forgotten some
of my nannies.

In 1939 my brother and I came to England, first of all
into a Quaker family, and then I was moved into a Baptist
one. I think I had a fairly normal upbringing there, with
the exception of being sent (as a day scholar) to a girls'
public school, which was a Catholic convent.

At school I was not the slightest bit aware sexually -
we didn't even discuss menstruation when it happened. So
I think my schooling was in a way asexual. The first awareness of things sexual came with my first career, which was
in nursing. I don't know why I was not at all curious
sexually - in fact I am quite curious to know why that was
so - but I just was not. I belonged to a mixed youth club,
and we did all kinds of things together, good healthy exer-
cise and walking, but never at that stage was there a boyfriend. I had crushes on women, sometimes fifteen or twenty
years older than myself, but I never thought of these
relationships as sexual - I just perceived them as friendships.

Being a nurse meant that at least I became aware of the
bodily functions. Also, there was an RAF camp next to the
hospital and the men were always dating the nurses. So I
found myself in couple situations and discovered very
quickly that this was not what I wanted: it was neither
satisfactory nor satisfying and it did not make me happy.
At the same time I fell desperately in love with another
nurse. I didn't know what label to put on it - other people
might have called it a crush - but I was in love. Of course
neither of us did anything about it. However, it was the
real beginning of my awareness that perhaps I was different
from my friends. I think it was at this stage that I began
to wonder whether I was gay, but I went through years of
alternately accepting and rejecting it. During this period
I became engaged to be married, but called it off in time.

I was very aware of the problems of the total Christian
commitment that I had made: my Christian witness and my
feelings about women did not fit together. My religious
hang-ups continued for quite some years. Perhaps my hang-
ups were worse than they might have been. After growing up
in a Jewish family, then a Quaker family followed by a
Baptist family who attended the local Methodist church,
attending a Roman Catholic school and Church of England Girl
Guides, then attending a Congregational church when nursing
and finally finding a home in the Society of Friends in the
1950s, it is little wonder that I had real problems! I
always wished and still do wish that the Churches would
preach their Gospel in a more loving way and discover for
themselves the liberating joy to be found in all the diversity of human experience.

I finally realised that I had to come to terms with my
religious inhibitions and my gayness if I wanted to escape
more years of dire misery. And I don't know whether the
answer I found for myself is the answer or just an excuse;

I just know that many other Christian gay men and women have
come to the same conclusion. I decided that love did not
mean just God, or me and man: it meant me and my fellow
human beings, which included women, and this was the only
way God's love could be for everybody. Also I realised that
in every human relationship God is there in the midst of it.

Now I was ready to experiment with relationships. I had
left nursing some years before and was far from settled,
but I entered into my first ongoing relationship at the age
of about thirty. It was a very liberating experience, and
I began to realise that I did not feel sinful about it. For
the first time I felt that in a relationship I could give
and receive, and for the first time it and I felt right.
After some time I tumbled into a somewhat hysterical relationship which lasted a bit longer. It had tremendous ups
and downs, which I suppose you have in any relationship; it
just felt like more downs than ups. It affected me more
than I realised then. I became someone that even I did not
recognise. I'm not even sure whether it was love.

At around that time I remember a wise Friend saying to
me that a relationship meant a good deal of responsibility,
and I should either accept that or stop playing around. This
was very much in my mind when I happily fell in love and
began a long-lasting relationship which continued for twelve
years and which unfortunately has now ceased. That experience gave me the knowledge that every relationship irrespec-
tive of sex is a very precious gift.

This wise elder Friend who gave me that advice - and
incidentally she knew that I was gay and had met at least
one of my previous partners - made, I think, a very important point. I believe that as far as responsibility is
concerned there is not a great deal of difference between
a heterosexual and a homosexual relationship, or between
long-term and short-term relationships. The only real
difference comes into it when there are children.

Once I was in my firm relationship I was given the confidence to come out to others as I had done to this elder
Friend with whom I have a very open and honest relationship: it was a great help and source of support for me
that she and my partner actually liked each other very much.
I remember as one of my best experiences that a few months
after X and I had started our relationship another Friend
dashed down to London and said, 'I've come to stay overnight
with you' and 'Bless you, my children'. It felt like a real
kind of Quaker blessing on the relationship and was very
profound. But you can always find your own Friend or Friends
to talk to - not necessarily from your meeting, just someone you trust and with whom you have a special kind of .
relationship. It doesn't have to be in a meeting for worship,
it can be anywhere - on the hearthrug in front of the fire.
Of course it would be good if Friends' Meetings would feel
they could give their blessing to gay unions if the people
involved so desired, because it would somehow make available
to a couple the support of the whole meeting. Gay couples
can be very isolated: they often don't have anyone except
each other to discuss difficulties with; I think this is a

59

responsibility for meetings to take.

Friends are in a unique situation because they are not bound by specific dogma: they have the freedom to think things through and use their heads and understanding. I find it somewhat strange that Friends are excellent at dealing with situations that are far away, but to deal with problems on their own doorstep makes some Friends worried and hesitant and immobile. I think that is partly because Friends find it very difficult to open themselves out and to let new ideas and new thoughts that are quite foreign to their nature flow about in their minds for a while.

Coming out to the Society as a whole was not so difficult after this. When David Blamires was writing his book Homosexuality from the Inside we had some working parties to help with certain sections, and it was only natural to come out to each other and to close Friends. And then we had the first meeting of FHF, when we formed the group, in Manchester with about twenty Friends present, and I think we realised that some of us had to come out if others were to know whom to contact. And although there were some doubts and questions in and around Friends House, there was also a lot of support. I don't think there's ever been a totally negative attitude. But I do think there is one attitude we have to get into Friends' heads - slowly but surely I think we are achieving this - and that is that homosexual does not mean male. I do resent having my existence ignored and I do feel that this is now happening to quite an extent. Whenever homosexual Friends' names crop up, they are invariably men, and we have to make Friends aware that there are many women - that they are around and that they are capable. In fact in FHF over a third of the members are women: a very high proportion compared with other gay groups.

Coming out both within the Society of Friends and more generally (and I do not want to separate the two) has meant a great deal to me. I do know that I am lucky in so far as I have always been openly gay in the firm of solicitors I work for, and that in the small town where I live my gayness, I feel, is known and an accepted fact. I don't particularly advertise the fact, but neither do I hide it. On occasions I have been invited to functions together with my partner and it has always happened as a matter of course. I think sometimes that if more gay people would be open naturally and not fight and not be over-sensitive about it they would achieve the same thing without the fight. But I do accept that if I were a teacher or had a job of that kind the situation might be quite different.

What do I hope for the next generation of gays? That they do not have to grow up with the hang-ups we grew up with, or go through years of misery before they come to terms with their sexuality, and that they do not face an actively discriminatory society. I think there will have to be a lot of legislative change. For instance I would like to see the age of consent the same for boys and girls, for gays and heterosexuals. And there will have to be some change to institutionalise gay unions legally so that they share the same benefits as heterosexual couples in taxation,

housing and so on. There can be real hardship if one partner
in a gay couple dies intestate and the family insists on
taking the estate so that the other partner is left with
nothing and sometimes homeless. I am convinced that there
must be changes here.

I am a woman, I am Jewish and I am gay: and of course
this means that I have been the victim of a good deal of
discrimination, a lot of it self-inflicted during the time
before I came out. About twenty-five years ago I had to
fight to get into the law because I was a woman and was not
a solicitor (I could have been a secretary or receptionist).
I am in England because I am Jewish and at school I was
either 'a rotten German' or 'a Jew who caused the war'. I
am gay, but it would take up several pages to detail the
discrimination that has caused. But it has all been part of
my own development, and in spite of everything I have been
and still am very fortunate.

16

I grew up into manhood before the Second World War and was
very much conditioned by those interwar years. I am married,
have one child and am unable to 'come out', so the reader
may now wonder what on earth I can have to say. But perhaps
some views and comments from an older man may be of some
interest if only to set another viewpoint.

The fact that this book has been printed at all is a
testimony to the real progress that has been made in bringing about a better treatment for homosexuals as a minority
group and I for one am deeply grateful to all those who
have worked for this, and have suffered insults and ill
treatment in helping those like me who did not know how to
begin to voice their needs.

I was brought up, the middle child of three, in a fairly
strict household. My parents were fundamentalist Christians
who did not mix with those outside their sect so that with
five years between each of the children I grew up fairly
lonely, reserved and shy, a great reader but with an enormous
inferiority complex. My brother and I indulged in the usual
boyhood sexual experiments and I had a cousin of my own age
with whom I had an occasional experience, but as they grew
up and began to be interested in girls, I did not. I missed
those experiences very much but had no idea how to find
them elsewhere and had no wish to try to have them with
girls. I put this down to my shyness and reserve, but later
on I met a girl of whom I grew very fond, and we married and
built up a wonderful relationship of loving consideration
and companionship in which we have been a great support to
each other.

But it was not until well after I was married and, indeed,
well into my thirties, that I came upon the works of
Havelock Ellis and others who made me aware of what the
various hitherto unexplained feelings, dissatisfactions and
particular interest in my own sex added up to. But there did

61

not seem to be anything I could do about it. I was married
with a child, had a career to make again after the war, and
I carried on meeting my responsibilities, outwardly fairly
mature and competent but inwardly a mass of frustrations,
of lonely dreamings, and, as I thought then, totally immature.

We joined the Society of Friends in the 1950s but it
was not untilI read the pamphlet Homosexuality from the
Inside by David Blamires that I realised that I was not
alone, that there were many others, and that all the guilt
and sense of immaturity I had felt those past years were
quite unnecessary. The relief was enormous. I could begin
to feel that I need no longer apologise for my existence,
that I needn't feel furtive and ashamed and as I gradually
came to know a few gays I realised that we were valuable
people in our own right, that we had a real contribution
to make to life, and I began to feel younger and more
positive than ever before. Since then I have come to terms
with myself, and know a little of what homosexuality really
means and the strong and beautiful experience it can be.

Although at my age and with my responsibilities I still
feel frustrated and despondent at times, at last I can feel
that I have found myself and can be myself. My wife and
child have accepted my gayness and it has not affected the
relationship which I value so highly. This makes me realise
that I am very much more blessed in many ways than those
who have not found a partner. I am not as free as they are
but one has to balance the benefits and the difficulties.
So looking back over the years I can assess what I have
missed and what I have gained. If they had been any different
would I have been any happier? for I have been very happy
on the whole.

Although I know that there is a lot still to be gained
I cannot help but wonder - as one who has to comment from
the sidelines - since we have achieved so much if we have
not reached a stage when we may ease up and consolidate
our gains and reduce the stridency of the demands and even
the bitterness which some show. Are we not asking for more
than many heterosexuals are able to enjoy? We are in danger
of creating a backlash, for despite the permissive society
it is not only those for whom Mary Whitehouse speaks whom
we have to fear but the over-fifties, heterosexuals of almost
my generation, many of whom are unhappily married but who,
because of the conditioning of their earlier years, are
more inclined to endure their lot however much they rail
against it privately, and who can be very jealous of the
freedom which we demand. I am sure that the attitude 'Why
should these poofs get away with doing what they want all
over the place when I'm stuck with the missus?' is very
strong in some areas. There are many older married men who
use gays to get the satisfaction they cannot obtain from
their wives but that does not mean that they are not contemptuous and resentful of the gays they use. Would we not be
wiser to soft-pedal our efforts for a while, to allow what
has been achieved to settle down into normal life? We want
to be accepted as ordinary people but we shall never achieve
this while we are stridently underlining the differences.

If we think also of all the disabled men and women,
particularly the younger ones, for whom sex is a closed
book almost, unable to talk about their sexual needs let
alone find ways of dealing with them, how much more fortunate
are we than they. I can't help but feel that we gays are
too concerned with what we want, with all the freedoms we
demand, instead of which as a minority we ought to be understanding and considerate of and for the needs of other
minorities. How high do we rate in our treatment of disabled
gays let alone the disabled heterosexuals? As an older man
I know how derisive and contemptuous the younger gay man
can be about bodies and faces which no longer bear the
bloom of golden youth, and I have seen the same attitude
towards those who have even a slight disability. I am
worried about the selfishness and egocentricity which is so
evident in the gay world. So many gays (see the advertisements in Gay News) seem interested only in youth, and seem
to want only that kind of sex, often paid for, the fleeting
contact and satisfaction only. Young gay men are just as
exploited and just as much sexual objects as women have ever
been. This may be natural - my eyes have gloated and my
hands have yearned to touch just as much as anyone else's -
but the vast majority are ordinary, the wrong shape, bald-
ing, wear spectacles and so on, and there are so many other
aspects we can look for that this selfish demand is not
only wrong but unnecessary.

I suppose that for men the sex act is such an immediate
reaction - we are so quickly aroused and our satisfaction
so easily reached - that we do tend to become engrossed in
our own needs and their fulfilment. A woman needs courtship,
the sense of being wanted and all kinds of gentle and not
so gentle stimuli to produce a satisfying and mutually
enjoyable result, whereas with two men arousal and some
kind of orgasm is almost immediate. Of course where each
spends time wooing the other and there is at least some
sense of delight and desire in each other the experience is
marvellous, but so many look only for a 'quickie' that one
begins to think they are the majority. We are not alone in
this; the insistence today on 'doing our own thing' has
sent us off course, and in all these demands for more and
more and in our rejection of mutual responsibilities and
our dependence on each other we are in danger of losing a
very valuable part of life. Some of the demands we make,
too, seem to me so trivial and unnecessary. Do we have to
kiss or otherwise caress our friends and/or lovers in the
street? These are parts of an intimate private life and to
be cherished as such, and are expressions of the sharing
which can be enjoyed.

Surely friendship is the most important thing. Friendship, sharing, common interests, mutual help and understanding; if these are present then sex is a glorious, exciting,
happy and laughter-making bonus. I am sure that this is
what we ought to look for, compatibility, an attraction of
spirit, not just the beauty of face or form. This is what
I would urge on the younger ones who have to grow old: not
just greed for the passing moment but mutual respect,

responsibility and consideration for others which is what
love is all about. This will endure when beauty is gone and
this will provide us with friends who in our old age will
comfort us and be real companions to keep at bay the
loneliness which so many dread.

17 Nick Chadwick

It is difficult for me to be quite sure when I first realised
that I was homosexual. I was certainly not one of those
fortunate enough to come to terms with their homosexuality
during their adolescence. Indeed, it is only in the last
few years, since the age of thirty, that I have attained
complete self-acceptance and freedom from feelings of guilt.
At the age of fourteen I became a Catholic, and at the time
fully accepted the Church's teaching on homosexuality. I now
realise that this coloured my attitude to my own awakening
sexual feelings in a decisive and inhibiting way.

It was one day when I was twenty-one, during my final
year as a student at the Royal College of Music, that the
thought came to me that I might be homosexual. It was a mere
notion, but a notion that resolutely refused to be dislodged.

For two years after leaving the College I was a research
student at Oxford. The segregation into single-sex colleges
of a large number of men and a comparatively small number of
women caused many of the men students I knew to be obsessed
with 'catching' women, and I was acutely aware that I could
not regard this as either pleasurable or desirable. The fact
that one of my Oxford friends was homosexual brought me
nearer than ever before to the point of 'coming out' as
homosexual myself. However, I still hoped that my sexual
inclinations were merely a phase that would pass.

The years that followed were, if anything, a retreat from
this position. Nevertheless, I believe that during three
years on the staff of Glasgow University between the ages
of twenty-seven and thirty I came to a measure of self-
acceptance, albeit while resigning myself to the prospect
of a sexually sterile bachelorhood, in accordance with
Catholic teaching.

At the age of thirty I moved back to London. About a year
later I entirely gave up my Catholicism, and it was at this
stage that I started to realise that one of the chief imped-
iments to my coming out was now removed. However, there was
still the problem of complete self-acceptance. Soon after
this, I found that, for the first time ever, I was able
to tell a friend of mine that I was homosexual.

When I was thirty-two I started attending my local
Quaker meeting, where I felt immediately at home. Imagine
my joy at discovering, on reading Towards a Quaker View of
Sex, that, unlike the Catholic Church, the Society of
Friends, with its faith in the validity of personal experi-
ence, could at least tolerate, if not always fully accept,
the likes of me. At a conference of Friends Homosexual
Fellowship almost two years later, one of the speakers on

the subject of 'coming out' so spoke to my condition that
the burden of guilt and unhappiness that I had carried with
me for so long completely fell away and has never returned.
I think I can truthfully say that this has been the crucial
spiritual experience of my life and that I am still living
under its influence. The purport of the speaker's message
<u>as it struck me</u> was the primacy of love. Since that occasion
I have learned by experience that within a loving partnership love and sex can confirm and strengthen each other in a
wonderful and wholly beneficial way. I never cease to be
thankful for the 'gift' of my gayness and the love that I am
able to receive, and, I hope, to give, as a result of it.

18

I have always known I was a lesbian, although I did not take
the word to myself until I was in my late teens. I used to
follow women in yellow dresses in my childhood - which was
quite a feat as I had to escape from the 'reins' and the
watchful eye of my nanny.
    I went to various boarding schools, fell in and out of
love with other girls ('crushes', they were called - 'you
grow out of them'): all very platonic and sometimes trauma-
tic. When I was fourteen I went to a school where I fell in
love with the Latin teacher. She did not know, but I was the
most hard-working student she had ever had, and I spent many
hours sweating over my books just to have her smile at me.
It was then, as my peers had grown out of 'crushes', that I
realised that my feelings for her were sexual. I started to
read about the women's movement and gay liberation; I also
read about lesbianism in some medical books which I found
at home, which painted a grim picture of a life of misery
ending in either suicide or alcoholism. I decided to take a
closer look. I hung around outside a gay club and saw women
in three-piece suits and women in 1950s dresses: looking at
myself I realised I was not in either of those moulds so I
decided to plunge into heterosexual activity to prove to
myself that I was 'normal'. I went on the pill, chose an
older man - better lovers, the media said - and lost my
virginity and my illusions. I came out to myself and to my
mother, who did not turn a hair, and was very supportive. I
started to come out to my friends; some of them rejected me,
but most said they had thought I was gay anyway. A middle-
aged Friend told my mother his son was gay, and through him
I met a lot of young gay people. I also got involved in the
women's movement, which gave me a new sense of identity and
a better understanding of the nature of oppression both of
women and homosexuals. I went to Art School, where I was high
on being an alive, gay woman. We demonstrated for gay rights,
for peace, wore flowers in our hair, sang and laughed our
way through school, books forgotten. I fell in love at a
peace vigil at the US Embassy: we made love not war for eighteen months. I had nearly finished my ceramics course when we
broke up and in spite of my grief I managed to finish it. I

decided to come to England to escape the memories of my
broken relationship.

I found my educational qualifications were not appropriate
for studying medicine, so I went back to school and emerged
a year later with six A levels and two O levels. It had been
a very good escape mechanism, the wounds were healed, and I
moved to London, where I rediscovered my zest for life and
joined Gay Switchboard, which gave me a wide experience of
the problems of gay people as well as a lot of insight into
myself. I made friends with many women and had another brief
relationship. When it ended it was time to take stock of
where I was going, and what I was going to do. I went to stay
with my brother, and applied to medical schools.

So I hung up my gay badges and started to live a double
life. I still have not openly come out to my meeting, for a
careless word in the wrong ears could put me on the dole.
After all, we all know gay people molest children, and lesbian doctors would take advantage of their women patients -
forgetting that male heterosexual doctors are in the same
position.

Sometime after Christmas in 1977 my mail caught up with
me, and after an exchange of postcards with a gay medical
student I had known in London we met at the Lesbian Conference in Bristol, where in spite of my reluctance to take on
an emotional commitment while I was a student, we fell in
love. The first few years of our relationship were difficult
as we were students at universities which were miles apart,
and then we had to survive D's house jobs.

When D got a job nearby, we lived in a cold, cramped,
damp flat and started to save up the deposit on a house.
All this time I was having exams every term and coming to
terms with the limitations of medicine, and D was working
long hours. Although our life style was rather hectic, our
relationship grew stronger and the end was in sight: I was
on the last leg of my course, we had found a house to be
our home, the future looked bright.

Disaster struck. I lost my vision and had to go into hospital for tests and steroid treatment: it was a terrible time
for both of us, as no-one could tell us if or how much I would
recover. When I came out of hospital I had to face the fact
that I might have to change direction and adapt to being partially sighted. I re-learnt to type - look no eyes! - and to
boil the kettle, and even how to pour out liquid without
spilling it. We got a dog so I would not be alone all day
(and now have three!). D was a tower of strength, although
we both knew she did not feel it. She encouraged me not to
feel depressed, and assured me that I would be able to lead
a useful life whatever happened. I put on as brave a face as
I could muster, but I cried when I was alone - the words
Multiple Sclerosis were engraved in fear on my mind. When I
first noticed improvement in my vision I thought I was delu-
ding myself, but it improved enough for me to go back to my
studies. I felt as though I had been to hell and back again,
but I could see and get on with living.

During my recovery phase we were finally able, after long
delays, to move into our house. But I was afraid that D had

been landed with more than she had bargained for, and, having visions of ending up as an incontinent wheelchair-bound burden, I was quite horrid to her, to give her an excuse to leave me. All the time I persisted in this misguided action D was very sweet and understanding, and convinced me that she loved me whatever happened in the future.

Since we have moved in we have been very busy decorating and doing the garden, and if all goes according to plan I will start my house jobs in August: we live from day to day. We are just beginning to be able to share our fears and anxiety about the future; until now we have been trying to sort out our own feelings and come to terms with the whole situation. However, we are both stronger people, with a feeling of the value of life and health and an understanding of how illness affects people which we did not learn from our medical courses. In many ways it is harder for me to come out as a person with MS than it was to come out as a lesbian. In 1981 the Archbishop of Canterbury said that, of the possible views of homosexuality, he was inclined to see it as a disability: I would like to inform Dr Runcie that my homosexuality is no handicap, rather that my lesbian relationship is a source of strength and courage to cope with my life - the pins and needles in my legs - and what is more, it gives me joy in life which I hope I can share with my patients: in other words, it is the living expression of my Quakerism. It causes me great sadness that I cannot come out to everyone I know, to let them see the source of strength, to have our relationship acknowledged - can you imagine what it would be like to have been married for five years and to have to pretend that you were only 'good friends', to have to cope with life's ups and downs without the support 'straight' couples expect as a right? To be afraid that a careless word could mean the loss of your job, house and financial security? The only handicap most gay people have is the lack of tolerance in our world, and those who would deny us our right to love. Which is why I still have to remain anonymous.

19 David Porter

My story begins in 1963 when, at the age of fifteen, I received counselling from the late Lotte Rosenberg, a child psychiatrist whom I later learnt to have also been both an active Friend in Winchester and a contributor to Towards a Quaker View of Sex, the now wellknown pamphlet published that year. I had been referred to Dr Rosenberg because of agoraphobia and similar symptoms precipitated by school examinations and when I changed schools most of these problems disappeared. However, it was she who first answered my many questions about homosexuality in a positive, constructive way. At that time I had little interest in sexuality but was acutely aware of my great affection for another boy, an attachment which lasted for much of the rest of my schooldays and which I remember as being one of the happiest

67

periods in my life.

Dr Rosenberg believed that boys were capable of much deeper friendship than girls. I don't know how true this is and have no wish to introduce gender rivalry into my essay. Nevertheless, I was later to enjoy numerous other close friendships with youths, many of them now married, and some of these relationships have stood the test of time.

During my teens most of my friends spent much time with me, and girls were of little interest to us. It was not until I had left school and had started my first job, in a South-ampton public library, that I had evidence of being 'different'. Some of my companions began to develop social lives involving girlfriends and a few of them even envied me because at work I was frequently surrounded by young ladies. I formed 'brotherly friendships' with some of the girls but did not otherwise feel particularly drawn towards them.

My knowledge of sex was considerably limited and I assumed that in the course of time I would 'meet a nice girl and settle down' as many others were doing. I was, however, very shy and introverted and was actually scared of some girls. I disapproved of the way in which a few literally flung themselves at men. I also felt that friendship was something to be earned; it could not be demanded as they were doing.

Some of my companions sometimes joked about 'queers', a race of sub-humans whom one was supposed to avoid at all costs. They told me of certain bars in Southampton that were frequented by such people, and one day I walked past one of these and tried to peer in to see what they looked like. I hoped that nobody would think I was one and I assumed that I was simply a 'late developer' and that eventually I would overcome my anxieties about girls.

The first major event in my 'gay career' occurred in 1967, the year not only of my twenty-first birthday but also of the passing of the Sexual Offences Act making male homosexuality legal, at least under certain conditions in England and Wales. By this time I had become very lonely and worried about my-self and had joined a psychotherapy group in London. This in fact brought little relief, for all I did was to sit week after week with several unhappy young people, some of them suicidal. One was a medical student with whom I struck up a friendship. It turned out that he was homosexual and was therefore the first gay person I had ever knowingly met. He was a well-educated youth and told me a great deal about gayness and gay life-styles, drawing upon his experiences of the London gay scene. In effect, he provided me with the information that had not been forthcoming from the psycho-therapy group, namely 'how to be gay'.

At first I felt panicky. I disliked such words as 'gay' and 'affair', thinking them to be more appropriate to a sleazy Paris café. I was also uncomfortable with the appa-rent eccentricities of that twilight world he described and wondered how I would fare. At least the fact that he was a medic and able to answer my questions about the physical side of homosexuality was something of a reassurance.

Eventually I left the psychotherapy group, largely through sheer boredom, although I kept in contact with my friend. He

68

and I spent a weekend together in Oxford and it was there
that we first enjoyed a sexual relationship. I was pleased
with the circumstances in which this took place. We were
both 'legal', we had already been friends with one another
for a couple of years, and it was I who in fact initiated
the activity. My story seems therefore a much happier one
than that of others who have had their first experiences of
gay sex in a lorry, or with someone they didn't know or
haven't seen since, or with a partner who treated them
badly.

The legalisation of homosexuality began to bring about
changes in public attitudes to gayness and one underground
newspaper started to publish advertisements for gay contacts.
At the recommendation of my friend, I decided to place one
myself. I received about two hundred replies over a period
of weeks and spent much of my time travelling around visiting some of these people. Many lived in London and in due
course I joined them there, accommodating myself in various
bedsitting rooms in different boroughs. It proved to be an
excellent way of learning London's Underground system and I
developed a life-long enthusiasm for railways as a result!

In 1969 I moved back to Southampton, my curiosity about
London's gay scene now satisfied. It was an odd period in my
life, for I gradually lost interest in gayness and continued
to maintain friendships with heterosexual youths. I had a
'crush' on a university student from Finland, a youth built
like a lumberjack but gentle as a kitten. He was engaged
to be married and when he returned home he sent me a photo-
graph of his wedding day.

I worked in the library at Southampton University and
sometimes during my lunch breaks would go cross-country running with a few of the students. When the academic year ended
I was saddened to see some of them go, for many had become
good companions to me. During this period a new problem began
to emerge, namely my feelings of discomfort towards young
women. I had rarely felt these towards older women but girls
still posed something of a threat. Some of the girls at the
library would stare and giggle at me, and one told me that
she considered me 'simple'. I presume they were baffled by
my lack of interest in them.

I reached a point where something had to be done. I re-
visited my medical friend in London and he suggested that I
contact an organisation that specialised in helping people
with sexual difficulties. I had become increasingly preoccupied with thoughts about homosexuality and hoped that
such an organisation might advise me. Why was I like this?
Was it true about possessive mothers, absent or inadequate
fathers, single-sex schools, childhood traumas, and so forth
producing gays? Why the word 'gay'? It didn't sound very
nice! And if homosexuality had always been with us why had
so little been said or written about it?

I made a day-trip to London and was interviewed by a
lady social worker. She recommended that I be seen by yet
another psychiatrist (by this time I had lost count of the
number I had visited) and also suggested that I attend a
recently formed gay social group in the East End. In 1970 I

69

paid my first visit accompanied by one of its organisers, a gay clergyman. The group proved to be most friendly and pleasant, and although in recent years it has been overshadowed by other gay gatherings I have always maintained a deep respect for it. In those days it was crowded with gay men and women from a wide area, although for several months I held the record in commuting, travelling from Southampton to London and back every Sunday!

It was not long before I decided to return to London and to take part in other gay activities, including the earliest meetings of the gay activist movement. I quickly mastered a rich social life, reinforced by some of the benefits of London. For the first time I experienced encounter groups, nudism and gay saunas. Gay London was at my feet!

Unfortunately the euphoria was soon to end. I met through one group a pleasant but lonely young man and shortly after we got an apartment together and became quite devoted to one another. However, his firm planned to open a branch in, of all places, Southampton and wanted to transfer him there. I was reluctant to leave London in order to join him, especially at this second point in my 'gay career', but at the time it seemed a logical step to take.

We found a flat in Southampton but our life there was a guilt-ridden one. We were so afraid of people finding out about us that when friends came around we would move the beds apart so that they wouldn't know that we slept together! I began to miss my gay friends in London but to say so simply made my friend feel inadequate. He disliked socialising and would usually leave it to me to make conversation with strangers. Our friendship gradually lost its sparkle, and after less than three years together we agreed to part. I felt a mixture of pain and relief: pain in that the break-up had caused me a great deal of unhappiness and loneliness, relief in that I had learnt that I was not yet ready for the strictures of gay domesticity and that I was now free to make a new life.

Prior to leaving London I had spent a few months as secretary of a gay youth group and used this experience in order to establish a similar group in Southampton. In 1972 the initial meetings were held in our flat and in time they grew considerably. I started the group from scratch and was its secretary for exactly three years. I arranged thirty-six guest speakers in as many months, including an MP, a journalist, a magistrate, a doctor, a radio broadcaster from the States, and various people well-known in the gay world at that time. I even got advertisements for the group placed in local newspapers and that alone was a tremendous breakthrough for the gay cause. I was in my element, organising the group with great enthusiasm! I also got to know an enormous number of gay men and women of all ages.

In 1975 I arranged the only public meeting on homosexuality ever to be held in Hampshire. It took place in Winchester and was attended by over sixty people including local journalists and someone from a nearby radio station. It was a very exciting event and one in which my whole self was involved. I only regretted that Dr Rosenberg, who had died two years earlier, had not been there to take part.

I was also responsible for establishing a gay befriending service in Salisbury, although the task of local organiser was eventually taken over by an older man who proved to be the right choice. My activist work continued until early 1976 when I started a group in Winchester similar to the Southampton branch, again organising it completely from nothing. Throughout that whole period I cannot recall any unpleasantness towards us. There were no threatening telephone calls, no disturbing letters, not even abuse at the many talks on homosexuality that some of us began to give to local organisations. I particularly recall being obliged to speak alone and without the use of a microphone to most of the first year students at Southampton University. My voice felt fragile for days afterwards! In those days it was difficult to share the work-load, and only a handful of group members ever involved themselves in gay activism. So often at that time it was left up to me to keep our ship afloat, but I enjoyed the challenge and for many months was indeed a winner with regard to our aims and aspirations.

I was not, however, prepared for the horrors that were to follow. The groups attracted many unhappy people. Some had been in prison or in trouble with the law, others had received questionable psychiatric treatments, and two of our members, one of them a clergyman, committed suicide. The arrival of a transsexual in the group caused quite a stir. Another whose behaviour provoked comment was a young man, scarcely out of his teens, who was so embittered that his conversation was frequently peppered with sarcasm. I wondered what had happened to make him like that. A third person who worried us was a middle-aged man, allegedly a gay Christian, who would cruelly criticise group meetings and who one day turned up at one with a black eye he had received from soliciting. Still in my twenties, I was ill-equipped to provide such people with either counselling or experience from my own life, and friends noticed how my personality had taken on a manic-depressive quality. I remember how once, when particularly miserable, I went to the local Samaritans and found myself being referred to - myself!

The year proved to be a difficult one in my life for it was overshadowed by a deep depression. The groups were largely unsuccessful as vehicles for campaigning, few new ideas were discussed, personality clashes stood out as important events, and there were no more public meetings. A Gay Switchboard was eventually established and was the first gay undertaking in Hampshire in which I was not directly involved. Yet somehow I boasted little interest in it, since it appeared to me that although switchboards could do excellent work in providing gays with information, counselling, legal advice and so forth, essentially they were little more than recruiting agencies for back-street bars where gays could be kept out of sight, or viewed with amusement by the tourists. Many of these bars had seductive, child-like names which created the impression that gay liberation was a kind of 'extended adolescence', a Peter Pan world of self-entertainment and consumerism that provided a startling contrast to

71

the women's movement in which there appeared to be greater emphasis on responsibility and determination. I became aware of how many gays regarded themselves and their fellows as children. One Southampton lesbian with a teenaged son would frequently and irritatingly refer to herself and her colleagues as 'all girls together'. Another man, at a gay meeting in Bournemouth attended largely by men well into middle age, would jokingly comment that he was 'distracted by all these gay boys'. There was even a gathering that flourished in Portsmouth for a few years known as BAGGS - the Boys and Girls Gay Society! And when the owner of a local gay club talked enthusiastically to one of these groups about his club's attractions I felt tempted to ask 'and when will you all grow up?'

I began to ignore the gay press, whose promotion of blasphemy, sarcasm, camp humour, in-jokes and unfunny cartoons suggested the work of mischievous but self-conscious schoolboys, and it seemed to me that one had to look towards other kinds of organisations to find guidance along the path to maturity. I recognised how some of the gay services were basically insulting to gay people in that they continually supported this 'Peter Pan syndrome' that I now found an obstacle in my psychological development. No wonder I had been depressed!

I noticed how much of gay liberation was still focused upon gays meeting one another rather than challenging the broader society with regard to its oppression or misunderstanding of gay people. All the groups I had been involved with had consisted entirely of gays and I knew of only one in the whole country that attempted to have an equal number of gays and heterosexuals in its membership.

I also became aware of the tremendous hold that the backstreet gay bars had upon gay people, especially outside London where there were few alternative gay gatherings. Even when a gay bar did not exist one had to be invented and the two campaigning groups I had started both eventually turned into gay pubs, a situation one can scarcely imagine happening within, say, the Campaign for Nuclear Disarmament or some other action-oriented organisation. Ironically, it was because of my fear and hatred of gay bars that I had started those groups in the first place. Discos were equally well-distributed, even though few gays I knew had anything to celebrate, and at risk of sounding facetious I evolved the term 'gay midas touch' to identify the compulsion with which many gays arranged events involving alcohol and pop music, a compulsion observable even amongst religious gay groups.

Other ideas came to me such as the fact that although the gay world by now had many methods for recruiting people into it, nobody had yet devised a means of getting them out again, by which I meant that whilst homosexuality is OK, the lifestyles based upon it could sometimes be questionable, especially if one got caught in them. I also believed that the willingness with which gays allowed themselves to be exploited financially was itself a form of self-oppression.

The 'way out', in effect the third and final point in my

'gay career', was shown to me by a gay girl, herself a birth-right Friend. She told me a little about Quakerism and one afternoon the two of us visited the Meeting House in Win-chester. I was impressed to meet local Friends and eventually in 1977 found my way to an Enquirers' Gathering at Charney Manor. The event served to be a turning point in my life. Unfortunately I was never able to thank its initiator for when her relationship with a younger girl broke up she became alcoholic and suddenly left Hampshire with no forward-ing address. I was greatly distressed by this as she and I had struck up a splendid platonic friendship, something quite new to me as far as women were concerned. I began to attend Quaker meetings regularly in various parts of the county and found these to be relaxing and healing. Quakerism opened up a new world for me, a spiritual dimension that had previously been hidden. I soon realised that Quakerism was what I had been seeking for years, and those silent meetings were a contrast to the rough and tumble of the back-street discos. My life took on a new meaning. I attended many meetings around the country and supported some of the fringe groups. By the end of 1979 I had become a member and in due course spent a term at Woodbrooke, the Quaker college. Nevertheless, it was not until going to Woodbrooke that I had had the courage to join Friends Homosexual Fellowship and then only after a great deal of reassurance from some of the staff and fellow-students that I was unlikely to encounter the same problems that had beset me in Hampshire.

At Woodbrooke I was able to reflect on past events and search for Quakerly concerns among them. I don't know how true my findings are, but I shall end my essay by present-ing them for consideration. During my peak as a gay activist I had published a letter in a local newspaper suggesting that one way in which gay men might be useful to society was for us to staff refuges for battered wives. The idea had been treated with scorn by the gays themselves, though I later learnt that Friends in Hampshire were at that time involved in establishing just such a hostel.

Similarly I had been, in 1975, the first person to write about disabled gays, a concern prompted by my friendship with a spastic gay youth and one which I'm sure Friends would have supported. My early writings were to have a far-reaching effect in the shaping of the national gay movement. More recently I've found that not only have many Friends shared my opinions but some have encouraged me to act on them. And so I've written an article on the dangers of sar-casm for the Young Quaker and another on the 'gay midas touch' for the Friends Temperance and Moral Welfare Union.

Finally, I am convinced that gay liberation is about 'gays getting back their membership of the human race' and that anything less than that misses the truth. In many ways I've now achieved that membership - I've made friends with families, children and heterosexuals in a way which was impossible all the time I remained in the back-street bars of Southampton. Maybe I'm rationalising, but it is Quakerism and not gay activism that has made me a winner, and I see no reason to change that.

73

20

Deftly, admiral, cast your fly
  Into the slow deep hover,
Till the wise old trout mistake and die;
  Salt are the deeps that cover
  The glittering fleets you led,
  White is your head.

How does a person come to be homosexual? Many answers have
been proposed, and perhaps the question isn't a very fruitful
one anyway, from an individual's point of view; but I'm
fairly sure that in my case it arises from my early family
background. I was born thirty years ago into a lower-middle-
class family in Manchester: my mother was over forty when I
was born, and my father had witnessed Queen Victoria's
diamond jubilee. I could hardly imagine them as having produced me, and they seemed more like old people who happened
to live in the same house - even now, to my great loss, I
feel very uncomfortable in the company of elderly people.
My father too had been in declining health since before I
was born, and I barely remember him as physically active.
That meant a declining family income, and after I was an
infant we never went away on holidays. I was an only child,
and we had scarcely any relations and saw them infrequently.
Family friends were few and while I was at school I suppose
I spent only a handful of nights away from home.
  So it was a lonely childhood. I was closer to my mother,
but my father's wishes dominated the household. He treated
me kindly and generously in his own way, but his idea of
bringing up children was one of stern discipline. I inheri-
ted his fiery temper along with his red hair (though I only
knew it as grey or white) and we had a very stormy relationship in which he often beat me with a bamboo garden cane.
It never occurred to me that there was anything unusual
about this. No opinions other than his were tolerated, and
since my views diverged at a pretty early age we had no
rational discussions - every conversation would turn into a
shouting match, a thrashing and tears. Soon there were no
conversations. This isolation and lack of serious inter-
change of ideas was more of a handicap than I realised: I am
still the worst talker I know. I had plenty of physiological
handicaps too, notably partial deafness; that's why now I
tell my married friends to start their families young or
not at all.
  Though there were few books in the house, my father - who
had knocked around the world and once worked in the American
gold mines - had intellectual ambitions for me, and persua-
ded me that I was a cut above the kids in our street. Being
able to sing Frère Jacques (without knowing what the words
meant) and recite the dates of all the English monarchs at
the age of about five were not really very useful social

accomplishments in terraced Manchester suburbia in the 1950s.
Not having a car or television or going to football matches
didn't help either. Of course I was ragged mercilessly at
school - I could always be relied on for a good tantrum -
and despite usual childish hobbies (toy trains, stamps,
astronomy), I was unhappy most of the time.

Well before I left primary school I was aware of finding
men's bodies attractive to look at - the dusty volumes of my
old encyclopedia still fall open at fuzzy photographs of
Greek statues - and the frequent changing, showering and
rugger-playing (the only sport I enjoyed) at my boys'
grammar school left me in no doubt where my sexual inclinations lay. I was (courtesy of the public library) a loath-
somely well-read child, and knew (or soon found out) about
Oscar Wilde, Rimbaud and Verlaine, Tschaikovsky, E M Forster
- though what they actually did in bed remained for some
time a mystery. My deafness had already accustomed me to the
idea of being a loner, an odd man out: indeed I was quite
excited at the prospect of joining another artistic and
intellectual elite, as it seemed. This is an important
point: I had no mental problems whatever in recognising
and coming to terms with my homosexuality. I never thought
about girls, and had no firends who were girls. Nowadays
half my very best friends are women, and I often get on
better - or more easily - with women than with men, straight
or gay: but physically I still, as I did then, find women's
bodies somehow strange or alien, like cats' or dogs'.

I was not pestered at home about having girlfriends - my
parents were simply not close enough to me to be able to
discuss my personal life or 'grown-up' topics of any kind:
indeed I don't think it ever occurred to my father that I
might have thoughts or a personality of my own. Sex was
never mentioned, and I had become a prude and a prig. I
wouldn't talk smut with my contemporaries, even with my
friends, such as they were, and if sex talk ever came up at
school I would bashfully shy away - another source of bait-
ing. Although physically I matured early I was very behind-
hand in becoming able to make any kind of sexual moves
towards others - I was just starting to have the courage to
grab at other boys' balls (as everyone had done in the first
form) when I realised, uneasily, that all the others had
stopped doing it. My father gave me a couple of confused
and mumbled sex talks when I was about thirteen (rather late
in the day). Masturbation, I remember him saying, was all
right occasionally, but he didn't have any respect for boys
who did it every night. If I felt like that I should try to
control myself, and to think of something that was quite
different, pleasant and neutral, like - like trout fishing
in Scotland. Since I hadn't been in Scotland since I was two
and had done no trout fishing nor wanted to, this was hardly
very useful advice - even if I'd been inclined to take it.

In most ways I suppose my adolescence was much the same
as that of many artistic 'scholarship boys'. I played in the
school orchestra and acted - despite a bad stammer I had at
this time - and wrote dreadful poetry. I was encouraged not
to participate in school trips abroad or in dangerous sports:

75

this cotton-wool treatment, I was well aware, was because I was a replacement (very much second-best) for my father's clever son by his first marriage, who had been killed in the war. It was never allowed that I might one day have tastes or grow up; and I chose to take a proud and superior attitude to this. If they don't bloody want me to smoke/ choose my own clothes/understand family finance, I told myself, I'll show them I can manage perfectly well otherwise. I'm not going begging to them or giving them the satisfaction of finding me smoking fags in secret. Thus did the self-denying perversity that has moulded so much of my subsequent life have an early start.

There was no religion and no church-going at home, so I was spared some traumas a lot of gay people have had; but I did get interested in my late teens in the phenomenon of religious experience and in biblical traditions, and briefly considered studying theology at university. I wanted to be a musician. Of course I thought about suicide a lot although as with most things I never got much further than thinking. When (some years later) the distinguished and much-loved musician David Munrow hanged himself I was shocked like everyone else but also rather comforted. It was reassuring to know that someone so successful could have problems too and also have the courage to give the world the ultimate two-finger gesture.

All this time I was getting my gay life vicariously through books, learning as much as I could, idolising people like Auden, Britten, Tippett. I spent most of my days - and nights - mentally undressing almost everybody, but was too inhibited to talk about sex - of any kind - at school. If someone had come up to me and said 'Hello, I'm homosexual; would you like to talk about it?' I believe I would not have hung back. But that never happened. Gay groups and counselling services were still in their infancy. I would walk quickly along Kennedy Street, where the national Campaign for Homosexual Equality office then was, glancing around furtively for a sign - it seemed appropriately seedy. To my father, queers were beyond the pale, along with murderers, spies, niggers, child molesters and those people from the BBC who wore suede shoes and green corduroy trousers. I found female impersonation and 'camp' wholly unappealing, and shuddered every week at Julian and Sandy in steam radio's Beyond Our Ken.

We got into the sixth form. The bully-boys seemed surprised to discover an element of something like tenderness in themselves, and we started calling each other by our first names. There was a boy I became friendly with who had come to the school only recently from an Oxford choir school, a year or two below me (and, I thought, considerably above me socially). He wasn't one of the subjects of my sexual fantasies, but I seemed to find myself bumping into him in the corridors a lot. We played Bach (and one of my own compositions!) in school concerts, visited each other's houses once or twice. He naturally had his friends in his own form, but I often wandered through the areas where his group forgathered, hoping to give him a wave or a smile. Then I left

school - and suddenly found myself with acute withdrawal
symptoms, crying and banging my head against the wall. Only
then did I realise that I'd gradually fallen in love with
him. (I didn't see him again, except once or twice in company, for ten years. Then he came back to Manchester - with
his girlfriend - and we have struck up an occasional drinking friendship, open but quite platonic, which I hope we
both enjoy.)

Off I went, full of confidence, to university. Here, I
thought, will be a sophisticated, candid and exciting atmosphere for people of all sexual persuasions. I was bitterly
disappointed. Cambridge prided itself on being forward-
looking academically: but when it came to matters of serious
human concern it turned out to be frivolous, class-ridden
and pretentious. The gay scene was completely underground -
this was in 1970 - and though there were a few openly gay
people, mostly upper-class and rather outrageous, there
weren't any at my college. One had to know the right people,
and I certainly didn't - I didn't even know whom to ask. I
felt alienated from the conventional sports-jacket-and-tie
brigade but had nothing in common with the opposite camp,
heavily into rock music and pot, who were doing most of the
interesting things. I quickly realised how wrong my parents
had been in considering me clever, and lost all my self-
confidence, though for reasons unconnected with sex. Eventually I wouldn't even go in the college bar, certainly not
on my own. I now think I was propositioned two or three
times by students: but by the time I'd said 'Pardon?' or
realised what was going on, the moment was past. In my third
year the gay scene became slightly more open, but by then I
was too repressed and miserable to take much interest.
Shortly before I left I plucked up courage to go to a gay
disco, something completely new for me, an experience both
terrifying and immensely exciting. In retrospect much of my
time at Cambridge seems to have been bathed in sunshine: but,
whether they're of wandering barefoot round the college
gardens, learning to see the beauty of pebbles and modern
paintings at Kettle's Yard, or crouching on the floor in a
foetal position in a corner of my rooms in the dark crooning
to myself to keep from crying - in most of my memories (and
certainly in most of the happier ones) I am alone.

In my second year I fell in love with a slightly older
man - one of the most brilliant students in my college, who
made a strong impression on everyone who knew him. This time
I realised what was happening, and sought out his company as
much as I could. I wasn't of much interest to him, and though
we met quite often I never felt I knew him well enough to be
able to confess my passion - and besides, he obviously preferred girls. The unhappiest period of my life so far came
at the end of my second year when, in the ten days or so
following my twenty-first birthday, I forced myself to see
that my love for Bill was hopeless; my father died; and I
had my first serious examinations.

Rather to my relief, Bill left, and next year the pattern
repeated itself, slightly less intensely, with a younger man
this time, whom I knew even less well. He never seemed to go

around with girls, and I've often since wondered about that.
By this time I was doing little or no work. The college
didn't want me to let it down in the examination league
tables, so I was packed off to the chaplain for hearty chats,
to the doctor for pills and to the student psychiatrist, who
seemed more interested in the number of O levels I had than
in helping me to solve my problems. I was immensely relieved
to get away from the place and its humiliating reminders
of wasted opportunity.

Back in Manchester with a poor degree, freed from my
father's oppression, and from the hectic social and intellectual pressure of Cambridge, I felt quite a lot better.
Gradually I began to come out to a few close friends, to
some college contemporaries, eventually to workmates and
others. Never in doing so over the years have I encountered
any real hostility. One or two acquaintances (mostly
'churchy' types) have stopped writing to me, and a few
others, while liberally tolerant, don't really understand
what being gay is about: but I've certainly not been threatened or insulted. Indeed to some of my straight friends my
gayness has seemed to make me a slightly less uninteresting
person to know. My attempt to join the Campaign for Homosexual Equality was frustrated partly by my diffidence,
partly by CHE's organisational inefficiency, but I went to
a few meetings of the gay group at the university, where
I was now working. I now knew where the local gay pubs were,
and very occasionally went in for a drink, mostly at lunch-
time or in the early evening when I 'happened' to find myself in the vicinity and therefore had an 'excuse'.

About this time the barriers came down between me and two
other boys, friends and neighbours since infancy (though at
different schools and colleges, when we slightly drifted
apart), who were also gay. I suppose the proximity of our
homes and families made us less than trustful. I started
the habit, which I maintain, of reading Gay News on the
train. I think this is socially and politically useful: but,
far from attracting other gay travellers, it seems to have
the effect of leaving one with plenty of space in a crowded
carriage! So matters have continued: I talk (reasonably
unselfconsciously by now) about my gayness to people who
want to get to know me on more than a casual or formal level.
I feel better for being much more open; and if my openness
helps to show even one person that we are not all effeminate
and promiscuous child-molesters going round in drag, then it
will have done some good.

It might seem as if, being more openly gay and having
quite a lot of gay friends, all my troubles would be over.
But there is a great difference between theory and practice.
Like other gay people, I wanted a stable relationship with
one person, and was prepared to wait a long time, as seemed
likely (considering the relatively small numbers of gay
people) if I relied upon strong friendships developing in a
natural way through work or hobbies in the predominantly
straight world. On the other hand, I didn't claim to be
any less interested in sex than other people and didn't
particularly want to be celibate perhaps for years. A life

78

of promiscuity and one-night stands doesn't appeal to me,
or to many others, but occasional short-term physical relationships entered into knowingly seemed to be far more
honest and positive than prostitution and no less natural
than masturbation. Kenneth Tynan once made a provocative
remark which I think it is helpful to quote in this context:
'Too many of us still accept the absurd notion that it's
wrong to fuck people you don't love, which is like saying
that it's wrong to travel except by Rolls-Royce' - and that
applies as much to gay as to straight people.

Eventually I did start having very infrequent sexual
encounters, mostly with people I knew rather than with
strangers. Some were enjoyable, some weren't; none were
repeated; and in half the cases the other men shied away
and have not seen me since. Partly this was due to a lack
of sexual confidence. I hadn't, in my over-sheltered youth,
had sexual experiments with other adolescents, or started
my active life as a gay person early enough to have the
advantages of immaturity on my side. So I didn't know what
to do: and as time went on it seemed to get harder to take
the initiative.

But these difficulties stem mainly from my deafness; both
the shyness and diffidence it tends to cause and the direct
problems of meeting new people, being an exciting conversa-
tionalist, picking up jokes, whispers, asides in environments
like bars, parties and discos - in short, of dealing effectively with the situations where most sexual signalling, of
any kind, goes on. I think this serves to highlight one of
the problems facing gay people. If I'd been heterosexual I
would probably still have been shy: but even so I think I
would have had little trouble in making friends and starting
relationships. It's easy for a man to get into conversation
with a woman, pay compliments to her and make his attraction
clear: women, however unfairly, are trained by society to
expect this and, to a certain degree, to tolerate it. It's
much more difficult, especially outside the context of
shared work or interests, to do the same with another man
whose sexual orientation you don't know. We are all aware
how trying to strike up a conversation in the enforced
proximity of bus or queue tends to be discouraged, so suspi-
cious have Eve's children become of each other. Even in a
gay bar or disco, taking the first step is a wild leap in
the dark. In my own case, too many shameful childhood
moments resulting from my deafness have made me acutely
over-sensitive to rebuffs or positions of embarrassment. So
I go on hoping that one day love may arise from some more
natural friendship which has a basis other than sex.

On the whole, I'm reasonably optimistic about the future
- things can, after all, only get better as far as sex is
concerned. I have a lot of friends, both straight and gay,
and FHF has in recent years played a large part in this.
Would I take the much-hypothesised pill to make me straight
in a flash? No - it's much too late now to learn new sexual
habits. I feel very positive about my gayness intellectually:
yet I am also conscious of happening to be a kind of person
not likely to make a success of that side of my life. This

79

love-hate attitude is only one aspect of the perverse life-style I see in myself: a (more or less) celibate sexual liberationist, a meat-eating vegetarian, a publisher who in some ways strongly disapproves of books... I am glad to see that younger gays are on the whole having a better time than I was ten years ago - and lucky not to have endured the longer periods of repression that some older gays have. So I have plenty of things to be thankful for. And after all, it is only the pursuit of happiness we are exhorted to, with no guarantee of any capture.

In Measure for Measure Claudio is imprisoned for having a sexual relationship with another person; and though he eventually wins through to fortune it is only after much anguish and fear for his life. But what's his crime? asks one of his friends, and another answers, Groping for trouts in a peculiar river. Maybe I should take another trip to Scotland.

21 Ian Noble

Hi! My name is Ian and I come from a middle-class family living in North Cheshire. I was educated at a private school near to my home and left with seven O levels and two A levels.

I had a happy childhood and loved school. In the first three years at secondary school I was rather an extrovert but as we all grew sexually aware I became more and more conscious of my gayness. I started to stand within the crowd, afraid of my friends recognising the 'poof-queer' syndrome that everyone talked and laughed about.

At school I had few close friends, but having always enjoyed my own company this didn't worry me. I loved all animals, taking a keen interest in biology and the surrounding countryside. So much so that when I left school, I worked for a year on a dairy farm and then went to college in Shropshire studying for an HND in agriculture. However, after a year on the course I decided to leave, as modern animal husbandry is based on profit margins, with little or no thought for the animals. Talking it over with my tutors and parents I decided to leave and study physiotherapy in Manchester.

Well, now that you know a little about me, I can tell you my story, which begins in Shropshire in the autumn of 1980.

At college I went out occasionally to Wolverhampton to go to the nearest gay club, and it was here that I met several people who are still close friends today. One night I went out to the club and saw a beautiful boy dancing with my friend Phil. I asked who he was. Rob was a little older than me, twenty-two to be exact, tall, with short black hair, skin-tight jeans and a T-shirt stretched over his muscled chest. Later on Rob came over to us and I was introduced. We chatted and danced and I was glad to hear that he was coming to the club the next week. I pumped Phil for as much

information about Rob as possible and the following week I
turned up dressed in black and white, Rob's favourite
colour scheme. We talked and danced and cuddled together all
night and arranged to meet the following Wednesday at a pub
in Shrewsbury where a few of Rob's friends usually met. One
thing led to another and before long we were going out regularly on Wednesday and Saturday nights.

At this time I was living in a flat with two straight
college friends. One went home each weekend, but Gary stayed
at the flat and was extremely anti-black and anti-gay. I had
tried to reason with him about his prejudices but I was also
rather worried about our friendship if he found out I was
gay. Anyway, I so wanted Rob to stay at the flat at weekends
that I gave Gary an excuse about transport difficulties.
After that, my weekends were shared with Rob (Gary seemed
not to mind), and our friendship and love deepened.

Christmas approached, and I was to go home for the vaca-
tion. My mother had known for over three months that I was
gay and after a while had accepted the situation. When I
first told her she was shocked, disappointed and said that
all I needed was will-power to pull me through this phase
in my life. However, after thinking over what I had told her
and reading books about homosexuality, she slowly began to
accept me. So much so that when I arrived home she asked if
I still had a boyfriend and invited Rob to our home for a
weekend. We were both thrilled: my parents made Rob very
welcome and I was pleased that they had accepted my relationship so well.

The weekend passed too quickly, but as soon as college
resumed I rushed back to Shropshire to see Rob. At this time
I was still deciding whether or not to leave college, and my
tutor said it was best to stay until Easter. I knew deep
down that agriculture was not for me, but it would also mean
leaving Rob behind. When I broke the news one night, he
started to cry, but the following week he asked if he could
come and live with me. This seemed a fantastic idea; when
Easter arrived we packed our bags and moved into a flat in
Whalley Range in Manchester.

Rob had not worked for eighteen months, but the cost of
the flat made it essential for us both to find work. Rob
found a job in a ktchen in a Wimpy Bar, and I as a manager
in a small fashion shop. Life seemed great as we were living
together, independent and in love. Rob loved the 'Big City'
with all the clubs and pubs, and soon we were going out most
nights. He hated walking, gardening, swimming, horse-riding
and animals; all of which I liked; but for Rob's love I was
prepared to give them all up. Rob also hated his work in the
kitchens and was soon moaning and complaining. In short,
life was not as rosy as we had expected.

We went to my parents' home some Sunday afternoons for an
hour or two, and they were always pleased to see us, but I
could feel that they were not happy with what I was doing.
I also had a feeling of guilt deep down inside me when I
talked to them. I felt that my parents blamed Rob for my
change in lifestyle. I had also stopped going to meeting,
and had not seen my grandparents as I knew how upset they

must be at me living with a man away from home. Even so, at the time I thought that my love for Rob was worth this isolation from my family and friends.

After a month or two Rob started to go home at weekends, feeling a bit homesick and also moaning about Manchester and praising Shrewsbury - the very opposite to his thoughts a few months previously. I still thought I loved Rob and was adamant in sacrificing all if necessary to keep him beside me. We had a great sex life, but apart from that the relationship was not getting closer; we were growing apart if anything. Our interests and hopes for the future were completely opposed: Rob was happy to have no job and to go out to the club each night, while I wanted job satisfaction, to go to college and to lead a varied and full life. Conflict after conflict ensued, until we even stopped having sex. At first I believed it was just a phase, and I kept saying that there was more to a relationship than just sex. This went on for a month and after a long discussion, Rob said that he looked upon me as a brother rather than a lover. I just screamed and cried for about two hours, realising that our relationship was over. In all this time we had both been faithful to each other, and I did try for the next two weeks to bring us closer together. It did not work; Rob said that he was going back to his parents and the dole. We had one last kiss and cuddle and then moved out of the flat. Owing to the distance we live apart I have not seen Rob since, but I wrote to him several times and he has telephoned me twice. I was not sorry at the beginning of the break-up, as I now had the opportunity of seeing more of my other friends and going out with them, which I had not wanted to do while I was with Rob. However, after a month the full impact hit me and for days I could not go to sleep without crying. It took about two months of worrying and hoping before I finally realised that it was best for us to part.

This sounds like a classic gay relationship - living together for several months, then parting, then both parties 'hitching up' again to another partner and so on and so forth. But for me this has not happened.

When I was with Rob I was deeply in love with him, in spite of our different interests and attitudes to life. Although I have had several lasting and fleeting affairs, Rob is the only gay person I have ever really loved: I had sacrificed a lot and got very little back. I still felt ashamed and guilty when I saw the people who had a deep and caring love for me: my parents, relatives, and Friends at meetings. I tried to avoid them; I even moved into a friend's house after the break-up as I felt that I could not face living at home. This guilt may be due to the gay urge to live as couples in this heterosexual society and prove to the world that we too can live stable domestic lives. I felt I had let my parents down and that it was just another of the flash-in-the-pan affairs often associated with gays.

Luckily my parents are very understanding and loving, and said that their home was always open to me, so I jumped at the chance and am still living there today. It was while I was at home that I was able to put my thoughts together and realise just who I am.

Before I moved back up to Manchester with Rob I was rather reserved in public, not wanting people to notice me, as I was only too aware of my gayness. While I lived with Rob, I became far more confident, even extrovert, especially at the clubs, and ended up flaunting my gayness. At different times I had lived the life of many gays, either closeted away or exhibitionist. Both ways of life are unnatural and artificial, and it has been whilst living at home that I have become myself again: the same person I was two years ago but with one major difference - I now accept my gayness. I am far more confident in public and am not worried about standing out from the crowd for fear of being recognised as an individual human being.

I still go out to the night-clubs to see my friends, but only about once a month, and I see my real, close friends about once a week, going to their houses, a pub, the theatre and so on. I have resumed all my hobbies and for the first time in my life I have real friends who care for me. When I was closeted I had no gay or straight friends. When I was in the clubs I had lots of artificial and insincere friends. I have also resumed going to meeting and have found friendship and love in FHF which has been a bonus to my involvement with Friends.

I will always look back at that time with sad and happy memories. I had jumped over the fence to find that the grass is not greener in the high-life world of clubs; it is only a fantasy world. I had many admirers, but a few exceptions apart, I found only opinionated, vain or else very lonely people ; but at least my curiosity was cured. This was also the time that I 'came out' to myself, and for that I am grateful. Now I can look forward to a life where I can accept my gayness with pride instead of shame, live among real friends, loving and understanding parents, and find joy in my heart for the happiness that being gay now gives me.

22 Jennifer Barraclough

My development into lesbian commonsense-hood is, of course, a lifetime's process. At thirty-six, I look back and remember the agonies of emotion I felt for Philippa and Patricia, two girls I first knew at primary school; I remained intensely aware of Philippa for much of my adolescence (which seems to have lasted until I was twenty-nine). I wanted to be liked, as many children do, but particularly by them. Philippa was a natural leader, something of a bully, and I ached to be chosen by her to play 'Grandmother's Footsteps' in the asphalted playground. I wanted Patricia to invite me to her home, a large rambling house with seldom-used attics in which several of us played doctors, and a comfortable living-room where I heard my first violin.

My friend was Casey, however, and I equally can't remember a time when a natural and easy love for her wasn't part of my thinking. We met when we were both three years old, in an orchard, wearing Churchill-style boiler suits, and through her I became part of the activities of a large family and of the small group of middle-class children in the village destined for 11+ success and grammar school. They would be the ones to catch the bus away to school, to carry satchels, to have homework, to leave for university, make money and come back home.

I belonged to the 11+ group because of my mother's capabilities and ambitions - she was a schoolteacher - but to the other group of children in the village, the labourers' children, the farm workers and the council house families, by virtue of my father and his family. After the war had ended, there were for my parents no job and no home - and my mother's pregnancy with me had put an end to hopes of emigration - so they came to Yorkshire, back to the village where my father had grown up. I went to the same school that he and his father had attended. We lived fifteen minutes' walk away from my grandparents' council house, in a camp of abandoned army Nissen huts with a lavatory block and no hot water, in a field, and were called squatters. It was an impossibly alien environment for my city-bred Welsh mother, who had gone away to college before the war. She received little support from my father's family and shared nothing with his mother except, I think, a terrible stubbornness. My grandmother was a working-class matriarch who knew that the mills gave girls a good living till they got married, and my grandfather had been a miner; I remember him now as thin, small and forever on his allotment or in his garden. My mother went back to teaching when I was two years old, taking me with her on her various supply jobs, to make sure we didn't stay in the camp. On my father's money as an unskilled fitter, we would never have left it, and never, without the astonishing gift of a piece of land in the village, moved into our own house. Now, in my own house, aware of the status and independence that means, I can understand better my mother's look of appalled disbelief when I once, not long ago, told her that as a child I had been very happy during the eight years of camp life.

She was always conscious of not belonging in Yorkshire. But I was conscious of adapting to both my groups and yet still not belonging. I played with Casey, and Philippa and Patricia, on their tennis courts and in their shrubberies, and hung around the village fish and chip shop on long summer evenings with anything up to thirty of the village children and the older, bored teenagers. Sometimes there'd be a wild, lemming-like race, all of us shrieking and tearing in a three-mile circular chase through our village, along the lanes, down the quarry, the length of the next village's main road, and back up the hill. The older boys always won, but I remember desperately making my ten-year-old self keep up with them over as much of the distance as possible.

It seemed, therefore, natural to be always slightly out of my depth. I had too much ambition for the one group, and not enough prospects and background for the other. But I was

at home at school. I liked school, right up to starting
grammar school. I used to do well, and feel comfortable
there. I wasn't very observant about Nature, and didn't
ever see more than 'Daisy' or 'Bird' for my nature diary
column, Things I Saw This Morning Coming to School; but I
got good marks for essays, was the best speller in the
school, had been reading since I was two, and, though slow,
coped fairly well with arithmetic. I liked the headmaster,
who once answered a question of mine about God's eternity
as carefully and seriously as he could. And I liked strok-
ing, very slowly, the inside arm of the girl who sat next
to me in class, whilst we had our Friday afternoon story.
Not surreptitiously, either, which is how I found out adults
didn't like us doing it. I liked Russell's black hair, and
Philippa's dark blonde hair. I seemed to have discovered
romance, and sent Rodney love letters which embarrassed him
a good deal. My mother told me I should never go into the
lavatory with another girl, and Susan and I - with whom I
was later to try on Tangee lipstick and draw eyebrow pencil
lines up the back of our legs for nylons - giggled behind
the door and wondered what she meant.

My reports from grammar school show a depressing downward
slide. At eleven, I was eager, tiresome, serious, willing
and emotionally under-nourished. By fifteen, according to
the reports, I was lazy, hostile, unresponsive, not ready to
work hard and under-achieving. I was still in the A stream,
but had given up entirely on maths and sciences and was
succeeding only in English and, intermittently, languages.
My reports said I didn't care: I cared terribly. They commented on my moods: I once swore to myself that I would never,
ever, say that my school days had been the happiest days of
my life. I considered suicide regularly and was preoccupied
with death. I was also wired up to, plugged in to, consumed
by heterosexuality. Like every other girl, I was being systematically groomed for marriage, being made persistently
and insidiously aware of my difference from boys and the
limitations of my gender, encouraged to achieve only in
careers which would allow me to become somebody else's
support and help.

And, unlike most of my contemporaries, I had become involved in a physical relationship with my cousin, a married
father who was then thirty-one to my thirteen and a half. It
was a relationship which was to continue, unbroken, through
my adolescence and university career, his separation from
his family, my parents' distress and disbelief, our marriage
and his eventual alcoholism, until I was twenty-nine and
walked out on what it had become one Friday evening in
February 1975.

At that point I was able to begin picking up some of the
threads of my own natural sexual and emotional development.

A recent American study has observed that sexual contact
with adults can bring about in the children involved 'subsequent behaviour (which is) bold, flaunting, even brazen...
Their interest in school work diminishes, they become preoccupied with sex, pay little attention to their homework
and are restless, inattentive and lazy'. I can identify

these characteristics quite well in my own adolescent behaviour. I was certainly a source of alarm to the boyfriends
I had of my own age, since I was much more actively involved than they were in sexual experimentation and rather
frighteningly demanding. My reports indicate the trouble I
was having at school. My relationship with my parents,
never wholly uncomplicated, became unmanageable, for me and
for them, and I recall feeling often that we were three
unconnected strangers under one roof. The effect of the
combined emotions of guilt and power in me was impossible
to cope with. I knew that I could never tell my parents
what at increasingly regular intervals over the years was
happening; at the same time, when I was chastised for more
acceptable misdemeanours, I could think, almost gleefully,
'But you don't have any idea what I really get up to!' and
feel myself in some obscure way their equal. I was also
wildly, perhaps necessarily, romantic about the whole
situation. As an over-read, intelligent teenager, I turned
the affair into Great Love, comparable only with Antony
and Cleopatra, or Tristan and Isolde. I had an only child's
over-developed sense of responsibility, too, and felt that
everything which happened was solely and utterly my fault,
my duty to live with, handle, be committed to. Quite what
my ex-husband thought about it all I have, I realise now
with some surprise, never known.

But the point which matters here is that it was more
than the actions of individuals which dictated this process.
It was also a product of the structures which surrounded
us, which in many ways supported and condoned this kind of
relationship. Adrienne Rich, the American lesbian poet,
writes more fully than I can of the question of compulsory
heterosexuality and its significance for women, but some
points are worth making. First, the assumption that heterosexuality is the norm. At a time when I might have discovered something about my attraction to either sex, I was
embarking on a relationship which society in many ways
encouraged. It was with a man, and I was female. It was
with an older man, and there were many examples of the
acceptability of that kind of age difference; and the alternative, older woman/younger man, attracted ridicule which
reinforced the other's rightness. Then, despite my mother's
active disparagement of early marriages, I was faced with
the constant example of her own marriage - she might have
waited until she was thirty, but she had done it nonetheless. (It is, as well, a successful marriage in many ways.)
And she was certainly aware of the need for male protection
in our society, perhaps because she was a working woman
and at that time, in that place, still unusual. Marriage
made her more acceptable. Everything I read seemed to
stress the rightness and inevitability of life with a
man - so what if I had anticipated it by a few years? Love
was in the air with a vengeance in the pop songs of the
1950s and 1960s, and in addition, I had grown into adolescence with the prevailing, if not wholly articulated,
attitude of postwar men, which I think was equally crucial:
that the war had been fought and won and the women were

86

their reward for surviving that dreadful experience. I had simply not had time to accumulate anything I could use as defences against all this, and so I was a ready participant.

It was not until I had found from somewhere the strength and courage to walk out of what the whole business had become, that I began to be aware of the resources which had, despite everything, been building up inside me through the years. It has been a slow and difficult (though rewarding) reconstruction for me. Unlike many of my friends, I was for instance deprived of diary-keeping, and could make no record, for fear of discovery, of any of the important events or thoughts of my growing up. So I remember now only in disconnected fragments, and sometimes through dreams: Ruth and Elizabeth, called 'lezzies' at school - in the brief moment before I refused to go on thinking about it at all, I smiled at them in a kind of envy. Frances, with whom I spent much of my time from eleven on, and with whom I have a recollection of love-making which refuses even now to surface and which neither of us is able to discuss. My ex-husband's unexplained anger over what he saw as my 'excessive' concern over my first teaching post, and the 'undue' influence of my headmistress there. A pang of unidentifiable emotion when one woman I knew in my twenties said, jokingly, of herself and another woman I liked very much, 'We're together so much people say we're lesbians' - the emotion was jealousy. The pleasure in teaching girls, the insistence on valuing their abilities, on persuading them to value themselves. Realising that I have in my life a long succession of women whom I admire and have in some ways tried to emulate - the head girl at school, Florence Nightingale, Eleanor Roosevelt, a friend at university, Susan B Anthony - and discovering that almost without exception they were women who derived much of their support and emotional wholeness from other women as well as from men (though when I read about them or talked to them, that fact was often glossed over, veiled or minimised). Being deeply amused, at about ten or eleven, when my mother, diplomatic but cautious, wanted me not to go to Guides because of 'funny women'. No explanation of why they might be funny. (I once asked her what gay men did; she looked uncomfortable and said, 'You'd better ask your father.' Not quite what she'd meant to imply! Of course, I didn't. I was too scared that sexual discussions would lead me to reveal too much, and so I held my parents at arm's length.)

My lesbian self in all these fragments struggling to survive - like Coleridge's sacred river, running unseen, underground, 'through caverns measureless to man'. And surfacing, when I was thirty, to combine with other, equally important, means of survival - my education, and my perception of religious faith. Because of my education, I was given the practical means of survival - I was able to earn my own living. (There were other benefits.) But when I had to shape my own life, I was able to pay my own bills. As for religion, it too flowed with varying force through my life, and shaped my concepts of morality, and the understanding I have come to of the relationship between human

87

experience and a recurrent knowledge of that whole which
both encompasses and is beyond humanity. From Congregational
chapel and Buddhism, through an abandonment of all formal
expression of faith because I could not find its relevance
to my own condition, I came to the Society of Friends half-
way through the year which began with the end of my
marriage and closed with the emergence of my lesbian self.
It was very much part of the same process of release and
growth. And it was also something to do with honesty and
practicality. I like what Emily Balch, Nobel peace prize
laureate, had to say about being a Friend: 'What is central
to the Friends is central to me - the wish to listen, to
understand as much as we can, and to try to live out, as
far as we can, all that one has of enlightenment - no creed,
no pretending to honour what we don't know.'
    I don't think of my first thirty years as wasted,
though I'm sometimes sad that I spent so long looking for
the right things in the wrong places. The difficulties
(and joys) of my teens and twenties meant that I was
without any of the guilt and anxiety which can accompany
realisation of one's gayness. I was so delighted to be
home at last, and had already experienced quite enough of
society's reaction to the unorthodox, that I was not vulnerable to those pressures. And to enjoy sexual behaviour
which finally made real sense, physically and morally,
was wonderful.
    It may be apparent that I am writing from the security
of a settled relationship. I can now put into practice much
of what I have been learning and feel confident about it.
I feel more than gratitude to the woman who was courageous
enough to bring me out, and deeply glad of the woman with
whom I now live. We have what I long wished to believe
could exist - a life together of equality, good humour and
mutual respect. We share a good deal, including our Quaker
faith, an inability to stop talking, a love of two impossible dogs, and a tendency to strong-minded self-righteous-
ness. We quarrel, we worry about money, we try to make of
our life nothing that will diminish us as individuals and
something that increases our capacity for growth together.
What we both know, finally, about ourselves is in Adrienne
Rich's 'Dream of a Common Language':

    two women together is a work
    nothing in civilisation has made simple
    two people together is a work
    heroic in its ordinariness.

Afterword

One of the most deeply held beliefs of the Society of
Friends is that of continuing revelation by the Holy
Spirit. We know that practices such as slave-owning and
slave-trading were at one time considered perfectly acceptable, though now we look upon them with abhorrence. We
know that music, dance, drama and painting were all
thought by Quakers to be vain and foolish pursuits. It is
clear that our values do change, and we believe, often as
a result of much prayerful thought, that they change for
the better. An immense change in society's attitude to all
sexual relationships has taken place in the last twenty
years and Friends need to consider carefully whether new
truth has come to light or whether, as some believe, standards have slipped. I believe that increasing knowledge due
to medical and psychological research has enabled us to
see the phenomenon of female and male homosexuality in a
new light. At this time, when Friends are encouraged to
search for new light on personal relationships, I believe
that the Society is right to expect that all Friends, men
and women, hetero- and homosexual, should think prayerfully
about every aspect of their relationships and try to see
whether they are in line with our Christian practice. It
seems clear that the Friends Homosexual Fellowship provides
a warm, caring group where such seeking can go on. The
acceptance and support it offers helps homosexuals to see
their lives in the context of Christianity.

Friends talk, sometimes too glibly, of seeing that of
God in all men/women. This book may make it easier for some
who read it to see that of God in the writers. Like other
Friends they are at different stages of the Way. Read and
re-read these contributions and you may be struck, as I
have been, by the exceptional quality of honesty shown by
almost all the writers. Perhaps one is first touched by the
unhappiness of the earlier years of so many of them. Loneliness and isolation, self-hate and guilt seem to be the
common experience. Noel Glynn has put it on record that he
grew up with a picture of 'queers as objects of derision,
pathetic characters, bitchy, mentally unbalanced, criminal
almost by definition, at best to be pitied, sad and lonely'.
What an indictment of society that young people can grow
up to feel that, simply as a result of their sexual orientation, this is the way society reacts to them! I doubt if
those of us who have not experienced these emotions can
imagine the bewilderment and even suicidal misery induced
by feeling such a despised minority. This most moving book
may open our eyes.

It happened that my own first experience of knowing a
homosexual was when I was told by a dear friend, whom I
greatly admired for his intelligence, artistic ability and
transparent goodness, that he was homosexual. My picture of
homosexuals has therefore been very different from the pre-
valent one. Subsequently I have found much to admire in all

those I have known to be homosexual, perhaps especially the remarkable honesty of those who have had to face and accept in themselves an orientation which they knew to be unpopular and often unacceptable to others. With great courage they have taken off the masks which nearly all of us hide behind. It may be that some things in this book will shock those who read it. Most of us have episodes in our past which we are now ashamed of and prefer to forget, but these writings show what devious ways people are forced into when they are afraid of society, afraid of being found out, afraid of never finding the love that everyone needs. We know that a starving person will steal or eat rotten food and we know that this is true of sexual needs as well. Far more important than the sordid descriptions are the almost ecstatic ones of at last finding acceptance and love and friendship after all the years of loneliness. In many cases this first experience of acceptance has been through the Friends Homosexual Fellowship. Nick Chadwick tells of the wonderful experience when 'the burden of guilt and unhappiness that I had carried with me for so long completely fell away and has never returned...the crucial spiritual experience of my life'. It is reminiscent of Christian in Pilgrim's Progress at the foot of the cross. Indeed, reading this book we are led through a sort of Pilgrim's Progress in the lives of many of the writers. Like all the rest of us, they are learning how to love, learning about companionship, understanding, friendship and eros, learning the place of each, and this is a lifetime's work for all of us.

It is clear from this book that Friends' meetings can do much to help. They can offer warm support to couples who have decided to try to spend their lives together - the same help and support that they would offer to married couples in the meeting. They can rejoice in the happiness of such couples. But like the two happy lesbians Christine Edwards and Valerie Grist my hope is that soon being gay will be as unimportant as being left-handed, and that the time will soon come when every gay will be accepted by the whole of society and all discussion of gayness will really be irrelevant.

Mary D E Guillemard

Some further reading

NON-FICTION

SIDNEY ABBOTT and BARBARA LOVE, Sappho Was a Right-On
   Woman, Stein and Day, New York 1972
NANCY AND CASEY ADAIR, The Word is Out, New Glide,
   New York 1978 (Short autobiographies)
JACK BABUSCIO, We Speak for Ourselves: Experiences in
   Homosexual Counselling, SPCK, London 1976
K C BARNES et al, Towards a Quaker View of Sex,
   Friends Home Service Committee, London 1963
LEONARD BARNETT, Homosexuality: Time to Tell the Truth,
   Gollancz, London 1975
CHRIS BEER, RONALD JEFFERY and TERRY MUNYARD, Gay Workers:
   Trade Unions and the Law, NCCL, London 1973
DAVID BLAMIRES, Homosexuality from the Inside, Friends
   Home Service Committee, London 1973
JOHN BOSWELL, Christianity, Social Tolerance and Homo-
   sexuality, Chicago University Press, Chicago and
   London 1979 (Now the definitive work on homosexuality
   from the ancient world to the Christian Middle Ages)
MICHAEL BURBRIDGE and JONATHAN WALTERS, Breaking the
   Silence: Gay Teenagers Speak for Themselves, Joint
   Council for Gay Teenagers, London 1981
CAMPAIGN FOR HOMOSEXUALITY, Queers Need Not Apply,
   CHE, London 1980 (A document on job discrimination)
STEVE COHEN et al, ed., The Law and Sexuality, Grass Roots
   Books, Manchester 1978
E M ETTORE, Lesbians, Women and Society, Routledge and
   Kegan Paul, London, Boston and Henley 1980
FAIRCHILD and HAYWOOD, Now That You Know, Harcourt Brace
   Jovanovich, New York 1980 (Especially recommended for
   parents and relatives)
LILIAN FADERMANN, Surpassing the Love of Men: Romantic
   Friendship and Love Between Women from the Renaissance
   to the Present, Junction Books, London 1981
JEANETTE FOSTER, Sex Variant Women in Literature, Diana
   Press, Baltimore 1975
GAY CHRISTIAN MOVEMENT, Exploring Lifestyles, Allison and
   Busby, London 1980
GAY LEFT COLLECTIVE, Homosexuality: Power and Politics,
   London 1980
GEORGE GORMAN, Introducing Quakers, Friends Home Service
   Committee, London
GEOFFREY HUBBARD, Quaker by Convincement, Penguin,
   London 1974
CARLA JAY and ALAN YOUNG, ed., After You're Out: Personal
   Experiences of Gay Men and Lesbian Women, Links Books,
   New York 1975
CARLA JAY and ALAN YOUNG, ed., Out of the Closet: Voices
   from Gay Liberation, Pyramid Books, New York 1974
JOINT COUNCIL FOR GAY TEENAGERS, I Know What I Am: Gay
   Teenagers and the Law, Liverpool 1980

MALCOLM MACOURT, ed,., Towards a Theology of Gay Liberation,
    SCM Press, London 1977
DEL MARTIN and PHYLLIS LYONS, Lesbian/Woman, Bantam Books,
    New York 1972
DON MILLIGAN, The Politics of Homosexuality, Pluto Press,
    London 1973
PAM MITCHELL, ed., Pink Triangles: Radical Perspectives on
    Gay Liberation, Alyson Publishing Co, Boston, Mass. 1980
NORMAN PITTENGER, Time for Consent, SCM Press, London 1967
KENNETH PLUMMER, ed., The Making of the Modern Homosexual,
    Hutchinson, London 1981
JON SNODGRASS, Readings for Men Against Sexism, Times Change,
    New York 1977
JULIA PENELOPE STANLEY and SUSAN J WOLFE, ed., The Coming
    Out Stories, Persephone Press, Watertown, Mass. 1980
ANGELA STEWART-PARK and JULES CASSIDY, We're Here: Conversa-
    tions with Lesbians, Quartet Books, London 1977
GINNY VIDA, ed., Our Right to Love: A Lesbian Resource Book,
    Prentice-Hall Inc, New Jersey 1978
JEFFREY WEEKS, Coming Out: Homosexual Politics in Britain
    from the 19th Century to the Present, Quartet Books,
    London 1977

FICTION AND AUTOBIOGRAPHIES

JAMES BALDWIN, Giovanni's Room   and other novels
DJUNA BARNES, Nightwood
RITA MAE BROWN, Rubyfruit Jungle   and other novels
GRAHAM CHAPMAN, A Liar's Autobiography
E M FORSTER, Maurice   and other novels
GAY MEN'S PRESS, Cracks in the Image (short stories)
JEAN GENET, Our Lady of the Flowers   and other novels
SUSAN HILL, Strange Meeting
ANDREW HOLLERAN, Dancer from the Dance
CHRISTOPHER ISHERWOOD, Christopher and his Kind
SEYMOUR KLEINBERG,ed., The Other Persuasion
JOHN LEHMAN, In the Purely Pagan Sense
ROBIN MAUGHAM, Escape from the Shadows
ISABEL MILLER, Patience and Sarah
KATE MILLETT, Sita
IRIS MURDOCH, A Fairly Honourable Defeat
PATRICIA NELL WARREN, The Front Runner   and other novels
BRIAN READE, Sexual Heretics: Male Homosexuality in English
    Literature from 1850 to 1900 (anthology)
DAVID REES, In the Tent   and other novels
MARY RENAULT, The Middle Mist (The Friendly Young Ladies)
            - The Persian Boy   and other novels
ADRIENNE RICH, A Wild Patience Has Taken Me This Far
    (lesbian poetry)
JANE RULE, Outlander (short stories)   and other novels
JOANNA RUSS, On Strike Against God   and other novels
KEITH VAUGHAN, Journals and Drawings
GORE VIDAL, The City and the Pillar
EDMUND WHITE, Nocturnes for the King of Naples
PATRICK WHITE, Flaws in the Glass
IAN YOUNG, ed., The Male Muse (gay poetry anthology)